PI SELLING

By
Cindy Manchester

COPYRIGHT INFORMATION

Published by Expert Message Group, LLC

Expert Message Group, LLC
5215 East 71st Street
Suite 1400
Tulsa, OK 74136

918.576.7306

www.expertmessagegroup.com

First Printing, May 2011

ISBN 9781936875016

Printed in the United States of America
Set in Baskerville 12/17.5

Cover design by Carlos Moreno, Auryn Creative

ACKNOWLEDGMENTS

Writing a book takes many people. Hugs and thanks to those who encouraged me to write this book and have given me their support through this process. My friends Marilyn Gates, Pat Nixon, Ruth Adams, and Theresa Stewart, your friendship, ideas and humor mean the world to me. The gals of EMG, Shari Alexander and Colleen McCarty, who got my vision in our first meeting. My fellow NSA (National Speakers Association) Oklahoma Chapter members, who supported my dream to write this book. Jean Kelley, who first introduced me to the personality styles. Tony Allessandra, whose work on personality styles has been an ongoing source of inspiration. To Josephine and Susan, the Duet Write team, words cannot express my gratitude for your dedication to this book and your uncanny ability to read my mind and color the pages with your eloquent words.

To all the people who have attended my training classes and aspired to become PIs, your stories have inspired me to help others.

Most of all to my husband, an aspiring P.I., Mark Salas, without your love and encouragement, this book would not have been written.

CONTENTS

INTRODUCTION

A s a real estate agent, there are so many things that you need to know about, from the schools and area attractions in the neighborhoods you're selling in, to mortgage and closing details. There's one other area that you need to add to your knowledge base as well: You need to know about people. All kinds of people. Because all kinds of people buy and sell houses, in order to get them to buy or list a house with you, you really have to know as much as you can about them.

Through your career in real estate, you've grown accustomed to regular contact with all sorts of personality types. At the end of a long day, it can feel as if you've encountered every single personality type there is.

The truth is, that feeling really might not be far off the mark. So, how do you figure out how to work with so many individual people, each with their own quirks, traits, wants and needs? You study them. Not each as an individual, but in categories, like you did when studying classifications for science or anthropology when you were in school. Except this is a whole lot more fun. You will be fascinated by the realization that while the expression "it takes all kinds" may seem to apply when you interact with the public every day, in reality, it takes only four kinds.

Believe it or not, all of the different personalities you encounter throughout your career can be narrowed down to four specific types, each with its own individual and distinct characteristics, not to mention pros and cons. Hey, nobody and no one type is perfect, though every individual, no matter the category they fall into, has thought that life would be so much easier if everyone were like them. Come on, admit it. You've thought that, too. But really, how boring would life be if we were all the same?

In your everyday personal life, it's perfectly possible and acceptable to surround yourself with only the types of people you choose to interact with. It's natural that you relate better to some people than to others. It's human nature. What's so great about the concept of personality types is that, by learning how to identify each of the four types, you can learn to successfully relate to – and better yet, in the case of your career, succeed with – each personality.

My instincts tell me that you're skeptical, wondering how that is possible. Can there really be a way to distill all of the seemingly disparate personalities you encounter each day down to only four types? The answer is a resounding "yes," and I hope that's got you thinking, "sign me up!" Because I'd love to show you what I've learned about identifying personality types and determining how to offer each one exactly what they need in order to close a sale. As an added bonus, knowing your own personality type and learning to identify those of others will be an asset in your personal relationships as well.

There are several systems for identifying personality traits, the most well-known being DISC, which identifies the four styles as Dominant, Influential, Steady and Conscientious. I've tweaked that acronym a bit and come up with my own definition for each type: Director, Influencer, Relator and Thinker. DIRT. That may sound strange, yet I don't think it is.

Here's why. I consider myself somewhat of a P.I., though not in the private investigator sense. I'm a Personality Identifier, who digs into a personality to determine which type it fits into and how to best relate to that person. In a way, I'm digging into the dirt, trying to solve the question of who the person is and what they need. Using the clues I uncover, I can formulate a sales plan and close the case.

INTRODUCTION

That's what I want to teach you – how to become your own Personality Identifier who knows how to follow the evidence to solve the mystery of your client's personality. You'll be amazed by how adept you will become at identifying the four types and deciphering how best to approach them.

As a realtor, you know the importance of developing a relationship with each client, trying to make a connection that allows them to feel at ease with you. I know of many realtors who have remained personal friends with clients long after the real estate deal was done. In fact, that kind of relationship building should be your goal, so that when your buyer becomes a seller or your seller a buyer, you're the one they turn to first. You also know the flip side, when you just can't seem to connect at all and you end up dreading each interaction. You may be doing what you think is your best; however, if your personalities are polar opposites, your best may be perceived as far less by the client. Meanwhile, you are thinking that there is simply no pleasing this person and that you just can't work with them anymore.

This book will show you how to work with just about anyone by becoming attuned to each person's inherent personality traits and adapting your approach to suit their needs. You'll learn to use the tools most valuable to a Private Investigator when trying to analyze and solve a case. Not magnifying glasses or recording devices, mini-cameras and other high-tech gadgets — though I'm sure they are quite fun — the tools a good Personality Identifier needs are far less expensive and way more accessible. All you really need are your five senses. Okay, taste, you might not need so much, but hopefully you get the point. By paying attention, observing, listening and sniffing out the clues people unknowingly leave all the time, you'll figure out how to best deal with them. How close does a client stand to you? Do they ask a lot of detailed questions? Are they warm and fuzzy or disciplined and professional? What tone of voice do they use? These and so many other physical observations can help you to alter your own behavior to fit with that of your client.

9

And I am here to tell you that it's entirely possible to do just that. In the pages of this book, you will learn the identifying traits of each of the four personality styles, with examples from my own experience to illustrate points along the way. I'll also discuss how generational differences have an impact on sales, and will teach you to recognize how a client from Generation X with a particular personality type has needs and expectations different from a baby boomer with the same personality traits. I think that by the time you're done digesting it all, you'll have second thoughts about the old adages "people are all the same" and "just be yourself."

Why take my word for it? What makes me think that the knowledge I've uncovered about the mystery of the human persona can change your life?

Let me tell you a bit about myself and the experience I've gained throughout my career that I'm so eager to share with you. Sometimes, the way people come into their business can be as important a story as the business itself. And to be honest, I've known since the age of ten that I was going to write a book one day. I originally thought it would be a novel about my family, but really, who'd want to read my life story? I promise to share only the pertinent highlights with you in the next couple of paragraphs.

I've spent the majority of my career working in sales, beginning with selling IT solutions and software. Speaking in front of people has always come naturally to me – I've hosted TV talk shows and one of my early dreams was to become a stand-up comic. I really, really wanted to be part of the *Saturday Night Live* cast. Although that plan didn't work out, along the way I met someone who persuaded me to study hypnosis. I'm not kidding; I am a certified hypnotist. Bet you don't meet one of those every day. And no, I cannot hypnotize you into buying into my theories through the pages of this book. I can, however, convince you.

I digress. In the early 1990s, when I was selling software to accountants and CFOs, I was invited by IBM to attend a mini-MBA program at the Wharton School. I found it interesting that the professors all talked about "relationship selling," which was the up-and-coming trend in sales at the time. It involved having a conversation with a client and developing a needs analysis, then figuring out a solution for their needs. As I listened to this "new" information, I realized that the professors were describing exactly what I was already doing. In fact, it was the only way I knew how to sell.

Here's what I mean. My personality is an Influencer. I'm all about getting to know a client through easy conversation and relaxed interactions. The people I was selling to were primarily numbers-oriented, and not exactly warm and fuzzy types. These clients weren't interested in shooting the breeze while we worked on a deal. They wanted facts – "Just the facts, ma'am," as Joe Friday would say (for those of you who might remember him) – they wanted figures and then they wanted to get back to their jobs. I learned that not only did I really need to do detailed research for them, I had to alter other aspects of my appearance and personality as well. Now, if you've been paying attention to some clues about me, you're probably not surprised that as a former hypnotist and wannabe comedian, I dress colorfully, if not eclectically, and I'm known for my bling. I also talk pretty fast and am very animated in my conversations. My sonar told me to tone down my appearance by dressing more conservatively; I slowed down my normally fast-paced speech and tried hard not to talk with my hands. In effect, I became more like my clients so that they would feel more comfortable with me. And it worked. They trusted me and wanted to continue to work with me because I focused on them and their needs.

Eventually, as happens to so many people, I needed to cut back on my business travel in order to stay closer to home and help my aging parents. My interest in sales and working with the public made real estate seem like a natural fit, and I received my license in 2000. Not to brag, but I sold a house the very day I got my license. With so much competition in the industry, that was a real confidence booster, and I sold to someone who was truly the exact opposite of my personality.

11

Since then I've earned my broker's license and today work as director of relocation services for my company, also hosting our firm's weekly television show and providing training to various organizations.

Throughout it all, whether working with a buyer or seller or leading a training session, I've used my DIRT system to make the most of each and every interaction. So in effect, I suppose you could say that I've added P.I. to my repertoire as well, since I view every relationship as an opportunity to get out my spyglass and dig into the DIRT.

Now I'd like to help you to become a P.I., too. Whether you're Nancy Drew or Sherlock Holmes, get ready to start digging. You're about to embark on an adventure that will change your life. Once you've learned this system, you'll find yourself applying it everywhere, and you'll be surprised at how rich and rewarding your relationships will become.

The Back Story of Personality Identification

Knowing the history behind personality identification might help to satisfy any nagging doubts you may have about its validity. The key to really understanding something or someone, from the principles of physics to the complexities of human behavior, is to know its history. The past can be a huge asset in predicting the future. As you learn the skills to become a Personality Identifier, you'll be able to anticipate your client's needs and reactions just as a good P.I. who cases a subject is able to calculate their next possible move. You simply have to know the history behind how a client's personality operates.

The origins of personality identification go back a long way, with roots as far back as 400 B.C. and the Greek "father of medicine," Hippocrates. While his concepts applied mainly to medicine, over time they translated to understanding human behavior. Following are the four temperaments of human personality according to Hippocrates.

Sanguine refers to the personality of people with the temperament of blood. They are represented by the season of spring (wet and hot) and the classical element of air. This personality is generally a light-hearted, fun-loving people person who is spontaneous and confident and loves to entertain. However, they can also be arrogant, cocky, indulgent and impulsive, and are prone to acting on their whims.

Choleric corresponds to the fluid of yellow bile and is represented by the season of summer (dry and hot), and the element of fire. This person is a doer and leader. While they are ambitious, energetic and passionate, they can be mean-spirited, angry and suspicious, expecting others to have the same approach as theirs and also dominating other behavioral styles.

Melancholic is the personality characterized by black bile and is associated with the season of fall (dry and cold) and the element earth. Often a perfectionist, this personality is very particular about what they want and, in some cases, how they want it. Kind and considerate, often overly preoccupied with the tragedy and cruelty in the world, they can become easily depressed.

Phlegmatic, which means "pertaining to phlegm," relates to the season of winter (wet and cold), and connotes the element of water. This personality is calm and unemotional, consistent, relaxed, rational, curious and observant. They are good administrators, though they have a shy personality and are often lazy and resistant to change.

Though Hippocrates may have been wrong about his theory that human bodily fluids influenced personalities, he adeptly cracked the code with the four-quadrant model. Galen, who pursued Hippocrates' theory many years later, changed the name of the model from the Four Temperaments to the Four Humors.

Upon close inspection, you'll discover that the behavioral traits associated with the four categories have very much the same characteristics as DIRT. I did change their order of appearance, though. Can you figure out which of the above corresponds with the Director, the Influencer, the Relator and the Thinker in the DIRT system?

Many, many years after Hippocrates and Galen, two other doctors, one a psychologist and the other a psychiatrist, were separately working on their own theories of behavioral styles and archetypes. Dr. William Marston wrote a book called *The Emotions of Normal People* and proposed the system and acronym of DISC. In addition, Carl Jung's research and theories led him to write *Psychological Types*, a book in which he proposed that there were eight different psychological behaviors based on the four mental functions people used most in their approach.

Sound complicated? Not when you think of how much more complex it would be to figure out people on a one-by-one basis.

Chapter 1
THE NITTY-GRITTY
OF DIRT

What you're not going to get in the pages of this book is a boring, textbook approach to learning the different personality types and how to identify which category your clients fit. Identifying someone's personality is fun. To have fun playing with DIRT, you've got to first learn the nitty-gritty of the system. Once you do, you'll be able to assess a client's personality and develop an effective and deal-closing sales plan.

When you deal with clients, whether they are buying or selling a home, it really is all about what they need. One of their primary needs is to trust you and to feel confident and comfortable with you. A person's home truly is their castle, and a real estate transaction is usually the biggest purchase – or sale – of their life. That means it's also an extremely emotional transaction, as well as financial. People need to sell or buy homes for various reasons, not all of them good. The family selling mom's house after her death; a divorced woman selling the home where she raised her kids; a family forced to downsize due to a job loss – these clients' needs and expectations are different from those of the happy newlywed couple or the newly promoted executive. Add into the mix the fact that each person brings their own individual personality to the table.

The bottom line is that the client is not going to change to accommodate your personality. They are who they are, and it's up to you to recognize who that is and work with them to close the deal.

Your life will really be much simpler when you embrace the concept that there are only four different types of people. The hundreds of millions of people walking the planet can be broken down into four distinct personality types. Each client who calls or walks into your office fits into one of these four categories.

I will prove to you that the categories of DIRT work (not nearly as complex as comprehending the concept of Einstein's Theory of Relativity, for example), and that it is a fascinating challenge that you will enjoy engaging in every time.

You'll learn the specifics of each personality type, how to pick up on the signals we all give out and how to adapt your own style to meet the needs of just about anyone. I hope this concept excites you, because I think it's amazing. Just think about the possibilities that playing with DIRT can open up for you. It's time to roll up your sleeves and dig in, get your hands dirty in the best possible way, the one that's going to change your business – and your life – for the better.

Caveat number one: This is not the same as judging a book by its cover. In fact, identifying someone's personality is not about judging at all. It's about observing and assessing, which are far more scientific in nature and pretty much devoid of emotion. The skills you will learn to apply as a P.I. will make you keenly aware of what clues and signals to look out for to help you objectively identify someone's personality.

Now, I'll admit that objectivity is a tricky thing. It implies being impartial and detached, which are probably the opposite of what you think you need to be when trying to figure out how to relate to someone. Haven't we always been taught that every relationship usually requires some type of emotional effort and input on our part? The key here is to first objectively figure out the clues that point to an individual's personality style and then move on to the relationship building.

The next key is that, once you think you've cracked the code to someone else's personality, you need to remain nonjudgmental. Think about how many people you've encountered whom you've made these or similar remarks about: "He's so arrogant and obnoxious," "She never talks to me; she's such a snob." Well, those are judgments. When you learn to throw judgment out the window because you now know how to look at behaviors as personality traits instead, you'll discover a huge difference in the number of clients you'll be able to effectively do business with.

Not because you can change them. People are who they are. While learning the DIRT system will give you a tremendous advantage in understanding people and building strong relationships, always remember that your goal isn't to try to change anyone. It's you who will be doing the changing. It's up to you to bend, because your clients are not going to. Your goal is to become aware of what to look for in a client to help you identify his or her personality, and then find a way to connect with them.

Now, before you start digging into everyone else's personality, it's a good idea to figure out just where you fit on the spectrum. Before you can bend to suit the style and needs of your client, you need to know yourself.

And, here's where that objectivity comes into play again. You may have to investigate your own personality far more objectively than that of any client. At this stage of your life, you no doubt have preconceived notions about who you are. What you learn about yourself may well turn out to be what you've known all along. Or, you may feel a bit like a double agent, thinking you were one personality type while being revealed as something else. There's no shame in digging up the dirt on yourself; as a matter of fact, the only real crime is not being honest with yourself. There's a certain confidence that comes with truly knowing *who* you are. I'm going to help you start to figure that out right now.

In the Appendix you will find the short version of a personality profile assessment I use during my training sessions. I have students complete the profile so they can get a better sense of themselves. This type of assessment is a great tool you can use to identify your clients' styles. It's also a very useful internal tool that works well in companies and corporations to help improve employee relations and team building. For now, let's focus on you.

I'd like you to look at the assessment now, as it will help you to figure out what your dominant and secondary styles are. Place a check mark next to each word that describes you and total the marks at the bottom. From experience, I know that some people are very reluctant to take this type of assessment. They don't believe they can be accurately assessed from words on a piece of paper. Or, they are going through a stage of life where their answers do not reflect who they normally are. The profile will only be as accurate as you are truthful. Just as a blood test doesn't sum up your overall health, think of the personality profile as a screening. If you decide to pursue your profile even further, more extensive assessments are available for purchase at www.personalityidentifier.com.

Look for the results of your profile test on the next page after the assessment in the Appendix. You'll see that you probably have a dominant type and a secondary style. You will learn all about the characteristics of your personality type as you continue with this book. Now, let's talk a little more about why it's so important to understand this information first.

Chances are that, as a salesperson, you're at least a bit of an extrovert. I'm an Influencer, which I believe is the reason I love sales and working closely with people. I absolutely love getting to know my clients, especially the ones I can be myself with, the ones who like taking time to talk over coffee about every aspect of a house. When I recognize that a client doesn't share my gregarious nature, I know that I have to tone it down and rein myself in a bit so that I don't come across as overwhelming or intimidating.

Whichever group you fall into, it's important to acknowledge the traits that are yours. If you are comfortable in your own skin, you'll be surprised by how easy it is to adapt to someone else's personality when you need to, which is the ultimate advantage of the DIRT system to your success as a realtor. You can reap the benefits most effectively when you fully understand who *you* are.

The accepted school of thought is that we are all pretty much who we are by the age of seven. Not in terms of maturity, or at least I hope not! Generally speaking, the traits that we've exhibited by that stage of our lives – whether forceful, optimistic, timid or cautious – are likely to remain our dominant personality traits into adulthood. For the most part, anyway. There are other factors, including culture and upbringing, that can alter an individual's inherent personality and how that person reacts to other personality types. You can't know what has happened in someone's past that has helped to shape their personality. And you don't need to know.

All you really need to know to be a successful Personality Identifier is who you are and how to recognize and unravel the clues that reveal someone's personality.

The more you incorporate being a P.I. into your real estate profession, the more clients you will attract. The more adept you become at being a P.I., the stronger your connections will be with your clients. The stronger your connections, the greater your number of sales and satisfied customers. The greater your number of sales, well, the more money you'll make. The greater your number of satisfied customers, the more referrals and repeat business you're likely to get. Need I go on?

If you want to learn how to be a good P.I., I guess I had better. That's the point of the book, after all. My goal is not merely to share DIRT, but to help you to dig a little deeper, pay more attention and be more aware about what to look for to better identify someone's personality. My goal is to give you a competitive edge.

Let's face it, the last couple of years have been hard on the real estate industry, and just about every agent and broker is facing the stiffest competition of their career. It may be a buyer's market, and you have to

19

remember that buyers are not only shopping for homes, they're shopping for realtors, too. If you can't make the connection your client needs, believe me, they'll move along to another agent. What's worse, they'll tell their friends that you didn't meet their needs; their friends will assume you can't meet their needs, and so on until you begin to realize that you're having trouble getting listings.

As a salesperson, you've surely heard the expression that people don't buy things, they buy expectations. I think this is especially true in real estate. A home is just about the biggest purchase any of us will ever make, and nearly every client you encounter brings an entire set of expectations to their search. For young buyers, it may be the dream of finding just the right house in just the right neighborhood to raise their family; an older couple may be looking for the perfect condo to live out their retirement years, a place where either will be comfortable living alone some day.

Sellers have expectations, too, especially if they're selling one home in anticipation of buying another. They want – and generally need – a specific price for their current home, and they also know what they expect from their new one. It's up to you to figure out what those expectations are and to find a way to help your client fulfill them.

Whether you're working with buyers or sellers, whether the goal is a swing set in the backyard or a high-rise condo, you know that it's invaluable to listen to your client and to maintain close contact with them. There's really no other way to have a successful working relationship. If you take the time to study the clues the client unconsciously drops, you'll not only understand their real estate needs, you'll have a better sense of how to approach them and how to adapt your style to suit their personality.

The following chapters will dig deep into each of the four styles; this is just a quick overview to give you an idea of their general characteristics:

- **Directors** are firm, confident and determined.
- **Influencers** are outgoing, enthusiastic clients who love to talk.

- **Relators** are concerned about relationships and may be slow to make decisions.
- **Thinkers** are self-controlled and cautious, and more analytical than emotional.

So what are these clues you should be looking for, the signs that will help you to determine which style someone belongs to? Use your eyes and ears to hone in on what the client is expressing, and you'll be on the right track to identifying their personality. Listen for verbal clues. A talkative client, one who appears to be an extrovert, is likely to be a Director or Influencer, since both are outgoing, fast-paced personalities. Introverts are quieter and more soft-spoken; Relators and Thinkers generally exhibit this trait.

You'll see visual clues, too. Directors will offer a firm handshake and steady eye contact, while Influencers are usually animated and may frequently touch you while they talk. Relators are slower and more tentative, and usually maintain intermittent eye contact. Thinkers are the most withdrawn, rarely touching and offering few facial expressions.

Are you having an "aha" moment right about now? I can almost guarantee that you've already assigned someone you know, be it a client or personal relation, into one of the four personality categories. You almost can't help it. And we haven't even scratched at the surface yet. So, if some of your identifier instincts are kicking in, that's great; just remember that like a good P.I., a Personality Identifier knows that one clue often leads to another, and that things aren't always what they seem. The more DIRT you know, the more perspective you'll have about your clients.

Digging deeper into someone's personality means that you're trying to figure out what they are all about. Like a good detective, a Personality Identifier needs more than just keen senses. You'll also have to pose the right questions – not necessarily to your clients, but to yourself about your clients. I've unearthed four key questions with the answers that apply to each personality type. What excites them? What is their greatest asset? What is their greatest failing? What is their greatest fear?

Using this as a guide, you will be able to categorize someone's style, at least on a preliminary basis. Remember not all is always as it seems, and using these four questions generically will help you get a read on your clients.

Clues:

1. The Director

What excites them?
Action.

What is their greatest asset?
They can out-accomplish anybody.

What is their greatest failing?
They can't stand weakness.

What is their greatest fear?
Being perceived as "soft."

2. The Influencer

What excites them?
Tossing around ideas.

What is their greatest asset?
They are fun to be around.

What is their greatest failing?
Being erratic.

What is their greatest fear?
Not being liked.

3. The Relator

What excites them?
A productive routine.

What is their greatest asset?
They are easy to get along with.

What is their greatest failing?
Timidity.

What is their greatest fear?
Sudden change.

4. The Thinker

What excites them?
Reason.

What is their greatest asset?
High-quality work.

What is their greatest failing?
Too critical.

What is their greatest fear?
Irrationality.

As you better understand the traits that are inherent with someone's personality, the less likely you will be to take any behavior that is in contrast with your own personality personally. No more agonizing hours trying to figure out why so-and-so doesn't like you or what you may have said or done wrong. Just chalk it up to their personality and use what you learn here to adapt and relate to them better.

Identifying your client's personality will go a long way in helping you to meet their needs, and there's also another factor that will strongly impact your ability to relate to them and meet their expectations. The generation gap is alive and well, spanning decades and cultures, which really isn't much of a surprise.

The three generations that are currently buying real estate are probably more different from one another than any earlier generations. With technology and a global economy, younger people have experiences and expectations far different from those of their parents.

Baby Boomers. Older baby boomers are from 55 to 64 years of age; many are interested in mixed-age living environments and walkable suburban town centers. Many younger boomers, who range in age from 46 to 54, are looking to move into their second home.

Generation X. These 33- to 44-year-olds are the cyber generation; they place a premium on instant access to information.

Generation Y. Also called Nexters, this group of 15- to 32-year-olds are children of baby boomers; most are more interested in renting than buying.

I believe that generational groups will shape the fortunes of the housing market over the next ten years. It's up to us to determine how we can accommodate their needs and expectations. As you prepare to show listings to different generations, the differences in their preferences are obvious, and the differences in their personalities are even more interesting. A retired CEO Boomer will require a vastly different approach than a high-power, rising corporate star of Generation Y. You'll take still a different direction with the more cautious wife of the CEO, even though they are of the same generation.

From this example alone, you see that with different age groups, different expectations and differing personalities, you've got a fascinating mix of clues to decipher!

No matter how good you get at using this system, you're bound to come up against a client or two whom you just can't make a connection with. When that happens, don't be judgmental – remember, they are who they are. And you are who you are, too. Instead of taking things to heart and feeling that the client doesn't like you personally, remember that there are some combinations, in science and in life, that just don't mix.

Your goal is to communicate more effectively to reduce any potential conflict. From there, you can decide how to work with clients who differ from your natural personality, or, if you indeed *want* to work with these clients. To be honest, I've had some high T (Thinker) clients who were a bit too detail-oriented for me to work with; we were both better off when I referred them to someone more comfortable working with that style. That's not to say that I would refer everyone in that personality style to another agent. There are just some cases where it's best. Ours is not to reason why. My role as a P.I. is not to figure out why we can't all just get along; what's in my client's or my own past or genetic makeup that stands in our way is not my focus. My role is to look for the clues, assess the personality and adapt to it, if I can.

If you simply can't get to that point, there's nothing wrong with referring the client to another agent. When you realize that nothing but frustration is going to result, cut your losses and move along. In the end, you and the client will both be better off.

Sometimes you only get so far, and the mystery behind who someone really is and why you can't connect with them remains a cold case.

Chapter 2
FOLLOW THE CLUES

D epending on your personality type, you may be feeling eager and ready to dive headfirst into figuring out someone's personality and seeing how good you are at it. Or, you may want more details to make sure you're doing it to the best of your ability. Whatever your own personality is, you can always dig in the DIRT.

If you were attending one of my training classes right now, after we'd talked about the four individual personality styles, I'd demonstrate interactions between various combinations, showing how each type can bend to better accommodate another.

What we discover by the end of our session is that most of the time your surveillance will turn up just the lead you need to get to the bottom of who it really is that you are working with.

Such was the case for Indie, a respected and trusted realtor to the rich and famous in the exclusive hills of Beverly. On a brutally hot afternoon, while she was focusing on the ice cooling her lemon-zested water, it was difficult not to focus on the ice of the clients to whom she'd soon be showing the most coveted listings in the city – and not the stuff that was cooling their cocktails.

Transport yourself to the swanky surroundings of the chic Bar Marmont, located in the legendary Chateau Marmont, one of the most historic hotels in Hollywood, favored for its privacy and castle-like appearance and ambiance. Frequented by stars and legends, diplomats and aristocrats, royalty and tycoons, it was relatively unknown to the general public and the kind of place where billion-dollar deals were sealed, where peace was sometimes made and sometimes lost. It was where Indie and her clients engaged in their first face-to-face encounter.

Though he'd chosen the location, Mr. Driver was seemingly oblivious to the surroundings, barely acknowledging the menu the waiter had handed him that was now lying closed by his side. He was impatient to get to the business at hand and scrutinized Indie as he sipped his cocktail. Of course, he'd had her thoroughly checked out by his people. He knew her background, including things about her childhood and education; he knew her reputation in the real estate industry; he knew her listings, her sales ratio, her average turnaround time for a sale; he knew the people she associated with, the kind of car she drove. He knew she was the best and it was imperative to his ultimate goal for him to be associated with the very best.

He was no stranger to huge and risky transactions, and this one had been meticulously planned.

Indie reflected on her first and only telephone conversation with Mr. Driver. His assistant, Relan, had made the preliminary phone calls, then he'd called her himself from his office in Aspen to make sure that they were on the same page before he and his wife made the trip to the pristine California coastline. The fact that he'd made the call himself might have surprised other, less experienced realtors; however, the phone call she received while pouring a much needed glass of wine after a long day of showings and closings didn't catch Indie off guard. As a P.I., she knew it made perfect sense.

His conversation with Indie had been straight and to the point. "I am aware of the details that you have already shared with Relan and am now ready to move forward. I plan to be in California on the fifth and want to ensure that you are available and prepared," was the extent of their conversation.

Thea, Mr. Driver's wife, sat to his left. A tycoon herself, she appeared quite comfortable in her lush surroundings, though her contribution to the conversation taking place at their isolated table in the corner was limited. Not that she was disinterested; quite to the contrary, she appeared to take everything in, absorbing every minute detail, even the waiter's in-depth descriptions of special menu items.

Sitting to Mr. Driver's right, casually perusing the menu and the view, was his personal assistant, Relan. He was a very comfortable, well-groomed young man who was easy on the eyes and easy to talk with as well. He ventured into conversation far more easily than Mrs. Driver; closing his menu mere moments after it had been placed in his hands, Relan had likely made up his mind about his meal before he even sat down at the table. He methodically unfolded the napkin to his left and carefully placed it on his lap.

Indie carefully and casually observed her new clients, taking mental notes about each while studying the lunch selections. Her initial conversation with Relan had been two weeks ago, and after gathering information from him about his employer, she'd done some research. First on the Drivers, then on all the possible listings that might pique their interest. Their assets were considerable, though Indie was savvy enough to know that this was only a small piece of the puzzle that would fit Mr. and Mrs. Driver into their new home.

Relan's presence at the lunch meeting was odd to Indie. She'd dealt with many high-profile clients, and though their assistants were sometimes in attendance at lunch meetings, they weren't as prominent in presence as he was. Something about his demeanor indicated to Indie that he was a key player in the couple's decision-making process.

Okay, this entire cast of characters, along with the story and setting I'm describing, are totally fictitious – and any resemblance to any actual person, place or thing, past, present or future, is purely coincidental. I have my reasons for making them up, and like any client, real or fictitious, there's more to them and the story than meets the eye.

That doesn't mean that what meets the eye isn't relevant though. Your eyes are one of your key assets for focusing in on the clues people leave behind that will give you a hint into their personality.

Let's take a look at the clients through the astute eyes of Indie, who, I'm sure you've ascertained, is a Personality Identifier. Each person at the table displays distinct behaviors and traits that will help Indie – and you – identify their personality. Even though we haven't fully explored the characteristics of each category, let's go back and analyze each person's actions and traits to see what we can come up with.

First off, did you notice all of the clues? Without reading ahead, jot down on a piece of paper what you observed:

Clues:

- Mr. Driver chose the location.
- Mr. Driver knew everything about Indie.
- Mr. Driver called Indie himself.
- Mr. Driver's conversation was direct and to the point.
- Mr. Driver's transaction was huge and risky.
- Mr. Driver seemed unconcerned about what he was eating for lunch.
- Thea Driver was not talkative.
- Thea Driver paid careful attention to details.
- Relan was friendly.
- Relan knew what he was ordering immediately.
- Relan was organized and methodical.

Without being thoroughly trained in personality identification, I'll bet that you were able to come up with a lot of information that gave you insight into these characters. Even if the realtor hadn't had an opportunity to do some background research on her clients, each one still exhibits traits that can help her figure out what they need from her. Juggling the personalities of clients isn't easy, especially when they are all involved in the same transaction. What's a realtor to do? Based on the clues, who should Indie pay attention to first?

The answer is that, really, her attention has to be divided among all three. It is the *type* of attention she provides to each that is most important to an overall successful relationship.

I sure learned that in a hurry the day the Moores walked through the door of the real estate office I worked in. Of all the realtors, in all the offices throughout the city of Tulsa...

I mentioned earlier that the very day I passed my real estate exam, I sold my first home. Well, the longer version of that is a bit more complicated than I made it sound. Here's the setting: me, the confident, newly licensed realtor ready to make my mark in my new profession; the Moores, a very nice looking older couple who informed me as they sat across my desk that they were relocating to Tulsa and wanted to buy a house.

I took in every detail, trying to ascertain their needs for a home and their needs as individuals. Mrs. Moore, very talkative, told me she volunteered in her community, mostly in the arts, and as I focused in on what she was saying, I began compiling listings to show the couple. She wanted to see pictures of the houses – the insides, the outsides, the dimensions of the rooms. Nodding as I clicked and printed, I was already convinced that I knew exactly what the couple was looking for. We talked amiably as I handed her a folder of listings with photos and all the details about a given house that she could want. But apparently not all the details Mr. Moore could want.

I could feel the air change as he carefully reviewed each house that had passed Mrs. Moore's approval. Mr. Moore was an engineer. Not only was he an engineer, he was a professor of engineering! While I had deciphered the clues in his wife's personality and knew well how to relate to her because she was an Influencer like me, I'd almost missed the hints about his personality. The big tip-off came with his questions. While she was figuring out where their furniture would go and how the grandkids would like the playroom she had planned for the upstairs, he was mostly concerned with how long the home had been on the market, the utility costs, the type of concrete used in the foundation.

I suppose it's true that opposites attract, which certainly makes it interesting and sometimes tricky to sell real estate.

Once I was clear on the Moores' individual needs and styles, the case of finding the ultimate home to suit them was closed. Well, almost. When we actually got to the closing table, Mr. Moore pulled out his HP calculator. With every eye on him and every eyebrow raised, he began going over every line on the settlement statement. Really, who does that? Even as an expert P.I., I thought, "Why does he need to do that? It has been gone over by several people and has to be correct!"

One and one-half hours later, Mr. Moore completed his inspection and actually found a $25 mistake in his favor. Hushed and silent during the fastidious process, the roomful of participants breathed in collective relief to move on with the proceedings. There were some grumblings later about the "waste of time" and "what's $25 in a six-figure deal?" but not by me. A good P.I. knows well enough not to judge. What I learned is that this personality style must go through the steps that they deem necessary to clarify and verify information.

In the end, you see, he did find $25. For him, it was worth the hour-and-a-half that it took. This personality type is so detail-oriented that they *must* research and check everything to make sure it is RIGHT, no matter how many times the information has already been checked and rechecked.

While at the time Mr. Moore pretty much drove me crazy with what I considered to be miniscule, nit-picking demands, I now understand that he really had no choice but to behave the way he did. Had I known this at the time, our interactions would have been quite different. Although in the end we both achieved our goals – he had his house and I had my sale – I would have been much less frustrated throughout the process if I had realized that his behavior was simply an inherent part of who he was.

That's not to say that I wouldn't still have felt some level of frustration. Recognizing personality differences is by far a tremendous help in building a positive working relationship, and as I've said before, people are who they are. The point is to use your P.I. skills to formulate the best plan for each client, particularly those whose personalities are vastly different from yours. It's a great way to make the best of every client relationship.

Here's something I'd like to remind you of: being a Personality Identifier will definitely help you to hone in on and learn to accommodate your clients' needs. Don't expect to fall in love with everyone you deal with. You are sure to make some friends along the way, and that's wonderful. But in some cases, your real estate sale will be the end of the relationship. Think back to our Beverly Hills story. From just the clues you already have, does it look like Indie and Mr. Driver are going to become friends? It's probably unlikely, although if she is able to adapt to his personality and meet what will surely be many demands, she might find herself with a repeat client rather than a new friend. For a salesperson, that's a very good thing.

Just remember to use your P.I. talents to make sure that each relationship is as positive as it possibly can be, and you'll find yourself with loyal clients and some strong recommendations for new listings.

Chapter 3
THE DIRECTOR

Now, back to our real estate story…

From our brief introduction to Mr. Driver in our fictitious tale, we already know that he is a classic Director personality type. In his meeting with Indie at Bar Marmont, it's clear that he is a person who naturally takes charge and assumes the lead. He is in the driver's seat, so to speak. He doesn't waste time, and does not have patience with people who do.

As a high D personality, Mr. Driver wants his business interactions to move at a fast pace. He needs to maintain control of a situation and ensure that his time is used to its maximum effect. That is why, although his assistant made the initial contact with Indie, Mr. Driver needed to call her directly to be sure that she understood what he expected of her. His phone call was brief, direct and to the point; no idle chit-chat or small talk. That doesn't mean he's rude or abrasive; he's simply on task and focused. His need to be in control is also the reason he chose the location for their meeting; he is clearly not a man who enjoys surprises or being in unfamiliar surroundings. His choice of such an exclusive location indicates that he can out-accomplish anybody, without needing to brag or boast about his accomplishments at all.

Some of this description might make Mr. Driver, and others like him, seem very formidable and unapproachable. While that may be true to an extent, it's important to remember not to cast a high D personality in a negative light. The reality is that Mr. Driver's personality is comprised of strong components that, added together, form a strong, decisive style. It is not negative. Though a high D may at times appear demanding, he doesn't see himself that way. He appears confident and self-assured, and yes, a bit intolerant of what he sees as frivolous wastes of time. Overall, though, Mr. Driver is a successful businessman because of his high D personality. Like many people who share his traits, he has focused on his strengths and used them to create a successful career.

As a realtor, how should Indie approach a client like Mr. Driver? We've already seen that she is a smart professional who knows the importance of understanding her client's personality. Just as Mr. Driver has learned all he needs to know about Indie, she has also been doing her own research on her new client. She knows that Mr. Driver is a leader in his field, running a Fortune 500 company that he built up from a small start-up twenty years earlier. From studying the company's annual reports, she has also learned that while he relies on his staff, he doesn't hesitate to replace employees who don't meet his standards.

Indie also knows that for Mr. Driver, this particular real estate transaction is about much more than just buying a house. The Drivers aren't moving to Beverly Hills solely for its posh reputation and high-profile residents. The house is actually secondary to Mr. Driver's primary purchase. In an effort to expand his corporate holdings, he is planning the takeover of a major competitor. It's a hugely risky undertaking; if it doesn't go as planned, it could cost Mr. Driver millions in losses.

To ensure that Mr. Driver feels comfortable working with her, Indie knows that she has to be brief, direct and to the point when she speaks with him. Without tipping her hand that she knows about his business dealings, she has to remain focused on presenting him with the information he needs without distracting him with anything that he would consider unnecessary. Mr. Driver wants facts and figures, and fully expects that Indie has done sufficient research to show him a selection of properties that match his requirements.

Of course, no amount of research can take the place of actually talking with Mr. Driver about what he's looking for in a house. Fortunately, Indie has learned enough about her client to know that she must carefully craft her questions and match her style to his in order to get the information she needs – and to keep him interested in working with her.

Indie has to come up with questions that ask "what" rather than "how."

"What is your price range?"

"What style home do you prefer?"

"What type of community do you want to live in?"

The directness of these questions will please Mr. Driver because he can provide factual, direct answers. On the other hand, questions that aren't clear or that lead to speculation will only serve to irritate him because he'll perceive them as a waste of time.

With that in mind, Indie knows that she shouldn't try to engage Mr. Driver in conversation about his feelings. As a high D, he doesn't make decisions based on feelings and will consider such questions to be pointless and off the mark. In addition, the things he'll want to know about the properties she shows him are factual, not fanciful. For example, he'll be interested in the house's price, age and condition – tangible, verifiable facts. He'll be much less interested in discussing the floor plan, the view from the kitchen, the landscaping. While those factors will all contribute to his decision, they don't carry enough weight to merit much conversation.

What Indie needs to do to make Mr. Driver aware of the softer aspects of the property is to highlight the logical benefits of each. Rather than asking him how he likes the extra seating area in the den, she should point out the advantage of having additional room for meetings. Instead of going on at length about the five-car garage, she can simply tell him that there is ample room for his motorcycle collection.

While a person with strong high D traits needs to be in control, it's important to remember that this doesn't mean they want to be surrounded by people who simply agree with everything they say. What they demand is facts and figures, not obsequiousness. What does this mean for Indie? She knows that when she agrees with something Mr. Driver says, she should agree with the fact rather than the speaker. In other words, Mr. Driver cares more that Indie accepts and agrees with his stated facts than that she agrees with him personally.

Every buyer – and realtor – wants a problem-free transaction. Yet no matter how much research Indie has done and how adept she is at accommodating her client, there are still bound to be some questions she can't immediately address or unexpected glitches along the way to closing. The truth is that sometimes buyers themselves don't know exactly what they are looking for, and only with the help of an expert realtor can they narrow their search for the home that will meet their every need. Having a heads-up on how to meet the needs of your client's personality will give you a tremendous edge in successfully matching them to the right home or finding them the right buyer.

Meanwhile, back at Bar Marmont, Indie couldn't help notice the brilliant glint from the flawless diamond on Mrs. Driver's ring finger as a ray of sunlight caught it just perfectly through the glass window. According to the information she'd dug up on them, the Drivers had been married for twenty years, and by all accounts, appeared to be happy together. At least there were no headlines or photos on Google indicating the contrary. In fact, there were very few headlines or photos of the Drivers at all...

Indie fought the instinct to comment on the weather outside, the ambiance inside or anything else that didn't pertain to the reason for this meeting. She had questions, and lots of them, as any good realtor should. Relan had emailed her details, to be sure, though Indie knew there was something more to this deal.

For a moment, she toyed with the idea of mentioning Mr. Driver's other business transaction that she'd read about online, hoping the conversation would lead to assurance that her hunches about which houses to show them were right.

"It might also prove to the Drivers that they made an excellent choice in contacting me for their real estate needs," she boasted silently. "When they realize how far I go to meet my clients' needs, they'll love me."

Indie's impulse is quite natural for an Influencer personality type. She loves talking with people, expressing her opinions, getting their input and yes, even showing off her knowledge and expertise a bit. She is still smart enough to remember the "**Platinum Rule**" of Personality Identification:

Do unto others as they would like to have done unto them.

The golden rule — do unto others as you would have them do unto you — is a beautiful, altruistic thing; however, when it comes to successful business results, when you want to relate and connect with clients in the best way possible, the platinum rule rules. Notice, with your acute P.I. skills, the difference between the two — in the golden rule, the emphasis is really on *you and the way you would want to be treated.* The platinum rule is all about the other person. Treat a client the way *they* would like to be treated, not the way you would like to be treated. If they want names and numbers, give them names and numbers. If they want ideas and stories, give them all you've got. If they want a handwritten list because they keep information in paper notebooks and folders rather than on hard drives and Word documents, brush up on your penmanship and write out that list.

Sometimes, adapting to the needs and personality styles of other people is asking a lot. While you are certainly entitled to be yourself, service-oriented businesses require you to accommodate your clients. Being what they need you to be can only help you to get what you want from them – be it the listing or the sale. You're not being phony; you're doing what you need to do to get the job done.

Wisely, Indie decided not to act on her whim. Although his big deal may have been prominent in Mr. Driver's mind, it was not the business at hand. He would consider any off-topic conversation an unnecessary deterrent.

Suppressing her usual tendency to query the waiter on some of the finer aspects of the culinary selections, Indie decisively ordered her meal, simultaneously making up her mind to be especially observant of each and every player in this deal. They were all so different, and she got the impression that each had a significant say and stake in this transaction.

"Excellent choice, ma'am," the waiter said to her. "That dish is one of my favorites. It's so simple and our chef uses only the freshest ingredients. In fact, there's one special feature in there that no one would ever think to use. We grow our own herbs, fruits and vegetables here. We're quite unique that way. Once you taste this, I promise you'll never order it anywhere else again." Indie smiled up at the young man, dying of curiosity about the special ingredient, though not inquiring further as she noticed Mr. Driver impatiently waiting to order. Another time, another place, she'd have this guy joining her and her companions for a drink by the time the meal was over. Though she could tell he was a kindred spirit, she had to curb her enthusiasm in deference to her client.

She already had her hands full trying to decipher the personalities that would solve the case of matching the Drivers to their perfect home.

As the others placed their orders, the waiter regaled them with details about their chosen dishes, going off on tangents and asking questions unrelated to the menu items.

Mr. Driver, who had been clear, concise and tolerant of the waiter when placing his order, had long since lost interest in his presence and conversation. Indie noted that his body language visibly changed, and though he wasn't rude or condescending, she sensed his irritation and dismissive attitude. Looking Mr. Driver straight in the eye, she smoothly transitioned from the waiter's small talk by commenting on the architecture of the building and immediately comparing it to that of some of the houses she was about to show him. A look that Indie interpreted as appreciation appeared on Mr. Driver's face. She knew that she had captured his attention. Now all she had to do was keep it.

As she reached into her briefcase, she saw the waiter turn back to their table and noticed Mr. Driver flinch as the waiter tapped his shoulder to inquire about something regarding his order. Ignoring the iPad on which she had downloaded photos and details about the listings she'd prepared, Indie instead pulled a crisp folder from her briefcase and removed a one-page itemized list of information to review with Mr. Driver.

Okay, it's homework time again. In the last chapter, you made a list of all the clues that gave you insight into the personality of each of the characters in our story. This assignment is even easier. See what a nice teacher I can be? All you have to do is make a list of everything that helped you decipher Mr. Driver's particular style. You already know that he's a high D, and you have probably come across many people just like him. What I want you to do is pinpoint the things he does that indicate his style. Jot down or highlight them right in the text. It's your book!

- Mr. Driver was impatient to order.
- Mr. Driver placed his order clearly and concisely.
- Mr. Driver lost interest in the waiter once he placed his order.
- Mr. Driver appreciated Indie's directness and attention to the business at hand.
- Mr. Driver did not like being touched.
- Now, take a look back and list the things his realtor did or didn't do out of respect for her client's personality.
- Indie did not engage in idle conversation with the waiter.
- She redirected conversation to suit the needs of her client.
- She chose a less high-tech means of presenting information.
- She suppressed her own instincts because she thought they were in direct contrast to Mr. Driver's.

Knowing that you have to be chameleon-like at times to adapt to your individual client is only half the battle. As a realtor, you need to know how their type likes to be treated. It's not always easy, though.

Have you ever been on floor duty and received a call about a property that went something like this:

"Hi, can you tell me the asking price for that house on Pine Boulevard?"

If that's the extent of the conversation and the caller speaks quickly, you can lay odds that the individual is a D personality. It really is possible, once you get the hang of this P.I. stuff, to peg a personality style over the phone. All he or she wants at that very moment is the price of that house. Time is of the essence to them and they don't want to engage in small talk. Therefore, when they call and ask for the price, just give it to them. They will be more likely to respect you and answer a follow-up question like, "Is that in your price range?" than to hang up on you. If you try to keep them on the phone, describing the home and giving information without giving the price, they will hang up and call someone else.

People like this are not rude and it isn't about liking you personally. When you think high D, think Donald Trump. Think adjectives like firm, forceful, confident, decisive and determined. Remember, "Just the facts ma'am."

When you interact with someone who is a high D, be prepared – they speak and move quickly. Step up your pace or they'll view you as weak or slow. Their time is very valuable (whose isn't?) and a D will show their impatience and intolerance for having it wasted. Be prepared with your facts and present them efficiently. I am known for making bulleted lists before talking with my high D clients. Rather than reams of paper filled with all kinds of details, high Ds delight in seeing those succinct bullet points.

When you show a property to a high D, emphasize the obvious factual benefits rather than the emotional ones. Those facts may be related to what your client's goals are, so be sure to address that in your conversation. "This house has a separate bedroom for each child and is in a highly sought after school district." If a problem should arise, discuss it in terms of how it will hamper their goal. "If we can't get this result, you won't be able to move in before the kids start school." Rather than complain about the problem or have you empathize with them, a high D wants to hear you offer ideas or solutions.

Keep your Director personality apprised of progress concerning their home. This style wants tangible evidence and factual information, such as a phone call indicating that the house has passed inspection or the closing is next week.

Have you ever called someone a "control freak?" They are probably a high D. Their need to maintain control could very well stem from their fear of being taken advantage of. When you are in agreement with a Director, agree with the facts rather than with them as a person. They are not seeking your personal approval.

Here's an important tip about dealing with the Director personality: While many people find it intimidating to interact with a person who is curt, direct and asks to-the-point questions, Directors welcome and respect others who treat them that way. You don't have to pussyfoot around this personality. As long as you know your information, you've got the goods.

Remember, though, that in addition to personality styles, there's another factor you need to throw into the mix of dealing with people, whether you're in the office, in the grocery store or at a social function. Age matters. The era someone grew up in influences who they are now.

You are probably not going to deal with a D personality of the Baby Boomer generation in the same way that you will deal with one who is a Gen Xer, and your interaction with a D client in their early 40s will differ from working with one in their late 20s.

As a rule, Boomers value competition, change and a good work ethic.

41

What your high D Boomer wants to see is that you are a hard worker who respects your clients' age and experience. Older Director-types may be frustrated by the use of current technology; while it may provide the efficiency this type demands, if they aren't familiar with email and online chat, don't try to communicate with them that way. Recall how our realtor, Indie, ignored her iPad and used less technological means to show Mr. Driver the listings she had compiled. Give your Director Boomers what they need in the way they are accustomed to receiving it. Usually, these big old dogs aren't interested in learning new tricks.

It's also tough for the Director Boomer to go from a sizeable home to an 1800- to 2400-square-foot townhome. While they are downsizing their home, they are not willing to downsize quality. Remember, this personality wants to know the logical benefits of their possible choices. Highlight the pluses of having one story or the master bedroom on the main floor; point out the pros of low maintenance by having a smaller home and yard. Boomers feel as though they are still young and Directors like to show off their accomplishments, so make sure that you emphasize the state-of-the art construction and amenities included so they can point those out to their friends and family.

In today's tough economy, Boomers have been hurt by lack of equity in their homes and an inability to retire. When you list a home for a D Boomer, you are going to have to give them some tough facts about the value and sales potential of their home. Remember this personality has concerns about being taken advantage of. Answer their questions as thoroughly as possible and when addressing problems, offer options and solutions. Be direct, and do so with respect.

You'll treat the Generation Xer with a D personality style much differently from a Boomer. Let's call this group DX. These are your clients between the ages of 33 and 44 who are entering their peak earning potential. As children of the cyber generation, they have always had access to information and highly value facts and details. This generation is accustomed to receiving feedback. Make sure the info you feed a DXer is factual, not emotional.

Since Ds like a fast pace, tangible evidence that progress is being made and time being saved, give the DXer websites and resources where they can access all the information you provide them with. You can be sure your DXer has already researched property values and thinks they know what their house is worth. They like being in control and are inherently skeptical; knowing where your information comes from will put them more at ease.

Xers do more interacting online than person-to-person; using email will probably be your primary communication tool with them. This works well for the DXer, since as a rule, D personality types do not have the greatest social skills. Show your DXer client homes that are of high quality and in move-in condition. No fixer-uppers for this group. They'll want to see floor plans since the layout of the house is of great importance. Point out to DXers certain aspects such as architectural details and energy efficiency ratings, in terms of what value they bring to the house.

The DY personality is between the ages of 15 and 32; they are largely the children of Baby Boomers. The Director from this generation isn't as skeptical, likes to see action behind words and doesn't mind challenges so long as solutions are readily offered rather than dwelling on the problem. The DY is young, and using humor goes a long way in interacting with them; just don't talk down to them.

Since they've never existed a day without high-end technology, you don't have to be Sherlock Holmes to figure out that you'll be communicating via email (some won't return a voicemail message!), text and other social media outlets quite often with your DY client who, as you already know, wants to be kept apprised of how things are going. Your DY client has visited numerous realty websites and perused dozens of listings on their own before deciding to work with you. Keeping your communications brief and to the point, highlighting modern amenities and technology, will satisfy this client.

Interestingly, these two younger generations see the benefits of exercise and staying fit. They often go to www.walkscore.com to see how an area rates in walkability. They want their kids to be able to walk to school and they, too, seek the ability to walk in their neighborhoods and communities.

The D personality of any generation doesn't have to stand for difficult. When you understand the classic traits of this style, you'll be able to accommodate them, no matter their needs or their age. Remember that three percent of the population are Ds.

Classic D Traits:

- Strong-willed and visionary
- Firm, forceful, confident, decisive, determined, risk takers
- Excited by action, compulsive need for change, thrive on opposition
- Speak and move quickly
- Greatest asset – born leaders, can out-accomplish anyone
- Greatest challenge – impatient with poor performance
- Biggest fear – being taken advantage of
- They appear to be impatient (and they are)
- Their time is very valuable
- They ask direct, short, to-the-point questions, which many people find intimidating

What the D Wants:

- Just the facts
- Tangible evidence of progress
- For things to move at a fast pace
- Results
- To know they have control of a situation
- To know that time is being saved

Dealing with a D

- Step up your pace or they'll see you as weak or slow
- Give a firm handshake
- Make steady and direct eye contact
- Maintain focus on goals
- Give the facts, nothing more
- Use bulleted lists when talking to a high D; hit the main points, give details if asked, make written presentations look professional
- Don't make idle conversation
- Ask "What" questions
- Point out obvious benefits of the property; nothing emotional
- Agree with facts rather than with them as a person
- When discussing problems, always address their goals and how those goals will be hindered
- Offer ideas or solutions; don't complain about the problem
- Keep them informed

Typical occupations of a D

- CEOs, Presidents
- Military leaders
- High administrators

Famous D Personalities

- Donald Trump
- Ted Turner
- William Shatner (Captain Kirk)
- Henry Ford
- Richard Nixon

Chapter 4
THE INFLUENCER

From what we already know about our realtor, Indie, we can see that she's clearly an Influencer. She is a people person, comfortable being front and center and always eager to meet new people and engage them in conversation. In a sense, those are great traits for realtors, who regularly interact with all types of people and have to be able to get out there and find listings and clients.

As a natural high I, Indie likes to establish a favorable, friendly environment by verbalizing her ideas. She works best when she can talk freely and truly enjoys working with people who share her penchant for conversation. Indie, and those who share her traits, are perhaps the easiest personality to identify. She's animated, often talking with her hands and using lots of expansive gestures. It's in her nature to reach out and touch the person she's talking with, and her handshake is likely to be two-handed. For Indie, it's a sign of her welcoming attitude – a high I is genuinely pleased to meet you and wants to express that right away. High I personalities love to talk. As much as they are comfortable talking about themselves, they also enjoy hearing other people's stories and usually try to draw people out. In short, a high I is the very essence of an extrovert.

As popular as Indie is among her friends for her fun-loving personality, she's smart enough to know that not everyone is comfortable with her outgoing, enthusiastic nature. As a professional, she practices the Platinum Rule, working to adapt her personality to suit each client. Her luncheon at Bar Marmont presents a challenge since she knows that, for whatever reasons, all three of her tablemates are factors in the transaction. That means that she needs to find a way to interact with Mr. and Mrs. Driver and Relan, all while maintaining a balance that keeps everyone satisfied.

The foursome maintained a pleasantly professional conversation while waiting for lunch to be served. Knowing that her clients valued information, Indie used the opportunity to tell the Drivers about the area they were planning to move to. She talked about demographics, local attractions and cultural opportunities, discreetly avoiding naming the names of the many rich and famous who already lived in the area.

As the party began their meal, Mr. Driver got to the point of the meeting.

"What do you have for me?" he asked Indie.

Putting down her fork, Indie looked him in the eye. "I have four properties that I think best suit your needs, with three more ready if you aren't pleased with the first group. They all fall within your price range and all are available for immediate viewing."

Mr. Driver smiled and nodded quickly. "Good. Which is first?"

For the next twenty minutes, Indie handed around the printed information on the four properties she had selected to show to the couple, describing each house in turn. In keeping with what she'd sensed about Mr. Driver, she cited facts such as price, square footage, tax rates – the details she knew would appeal to him.

There was one thing about the Drivers' list of "must haves" for their new home that puzzled Indie. The first item on their list was a separate guesthouse. Indie knew that Mr. and Mrs. Driver did not have children. They were looking at huge homes with at least four bedrooms, which would seem to provide plenty of room for guests, yet they insisted on a two-bedroom guesthouse as well. It seemed strange that they would want to spend extra money on what didn't seem like a necessity, especially in light of Mr. Driver's pending business deal. The guesthouse was clearly a deal breaker, though, so she knew better than to question their reasons.

After the plates were cleared and everyone had ordered coffee, Indie heard a familiar voice calling her name. Ima Partay, a client for whom Indie was about to sell a multimillion dollar property, was fast approaching the table.

"Indie, what a treat to see you here!" Ima exclaimed as she enveloped Indie in a friendly hug. "I'm having a late lunch with my sister; she's come in to visit from Chicago; we haven't seen one another in…"

Indie experienced a moment of panic. She truly felt caught between a rock and a hard place – Mr. Driver, her prospective client, on one side, and Ima Partay, her current client, on the other. At any other time, she'd love to hear about Ima's sister and what the two women had planned while she was in town. Today, she knew that taking her attention away from Mr. Driver to talk with Ima could cost her this new client, yet how could she be rude to Ima, with whom she'd already established a friendly relationship?

Indie thought quickly. Technically, Ima was encroaching on Mr. Driver's time, and she needed a tactful way to make that clear without offending Ima or taking too much time away from the Drivers.

Indie took Ima's hand in hers and, looking straight at Mr. Driver said, "Mr. Driver, I'd like to introduce my client, Ima Partay. And this is Mrs. Driver, and their assistant Relan Rogers."

Mr. Driver said a polite hello and Indie addressed Ms. Partay. "Ima, I'm so pleased to see you; I'll call you this afternoon to go over the details of your closing. Does that work for you?"

With Indie still touching her hand, Ima understood that her realtor wasn't able to engage in small talk at the moment. She said a round of polite yet friendly goodbyes before returning to her own table.

Given her nature, Indie wanted to apologize for the interruption and explain that Ima was excited about her rapidly approaching closing and liked to talk about what she was doing. Yet despite her nature, she knew that Mr. Driver had been displeased with Ima's interruption. He didn't care about the reason; he wasn't interested in Ima. Once she left the table, he was ready to get back to the business at hand. Any attempt on Indie's part to explain away the interruption would have been extraneous, just a further delay.

Instead of talking about Ima, Indie said to Mr. Driver, "I apologize for the brief interruption. Now, what other questions can I answer for you?"

As the meeting progresses, we're finding more clues you can use to solve the mystery of each player's personality. Here's what's happened so far:

- The Drivers insisted on having a guesthouse.
- The Drivers do not have children.
- Ima Partay felt comfortable approaching Indie's table.
- Ima talked easily about herself and her plans.
- Ima understood that Indie couldn't devote time to her.

Are you also keeping track of Indie's responses to these clues? She has:

- Given Mr. Driver the information he needs despite her questions.
- Deftly handled an unexpected interruption by a high I client.
- Kept the meeting on track following Ima's appearance.

That last clue might just be the best thing that Indie could have done. When Ima Partay approaches the table, Indie finds herself faced with a fellow high I. Though she enjoys working with Ima, in large part because of their similarities, she knows that this is not the time for friendly chatter. Indie has to do some fast thinking to figure out how to let Ima know that she is interrupting a meeting while simultaneously keeping Mr. Driver from being annoyed by the interruption. Though she clearly has the P.I. skills needed to recognize the situation, Indie proves her abilities by diplomatically defusing the situation and keeping both clients happy.

She reflected on just how different this meeting with Mr. Driver was from her first encounter with Ima. On a busy afternoon two months earlier, Indie answered a phone call in her office.

"Premier Properties Limited. This is Indie; how may I help you?"

"Oh hello, Indie. This is Ima Partay. I live over in Beverly Estates and I want to sell my house. Well, I don't really want to sell it. My kids are all grown now and I'm just rambling around this big place by myself. With them all over the country – my son's in Atlanta and my girls are in Dallas and New York – I figure it's time to whittle down the square footage a bit."

"I'd love to help you, Ima. I can certainly see how you might want to downsize with your children all living far away. Where are you planning to move to?"

"Well, since the kids are scattered around the country, I think I'll stay around here, just in something smaller. Maybe a nice condo that I don't have to keep up myself. Since my husband passed on two years ago, I've been responsible for all the maintenance on the house. Though I have people to do it, I'm paying them a small fortune!"

"I can certainly understand that," Indie agreed, making a note to start compiling a list of condos for Ms. Partay to look at. "Where are you located in Beverly Estates?"

"I'm on West Hill, right off Skylark. It's number 17810, green with a gabled roof. I do love this house, I'll tell you. My kids all grew up here; I swear every room's got a story. Oh, the parties we've had! My husband was a film editor, and we loved to entertain. Honey, I could name some names! And after we had the backyard redone five years ago, with the outdoor kitchen and fire pit, it seemed like the fun just never ended."

The call continued in much the same vein. After the two women talked amiably for several more minutes, they agreed that Indie would visit Ima's home the following morning.

You can see how very different this call is from Indie's first contact with Mr. Driver, which lasted mere minutes and never veered off track. They're worlds apart, yet this one also left Indie with some solid clues about her new client. From Ima's outgoing, friendly call, Indie knew immediately that she was a high I. Here are the clues Ima left without even realizing it:

- She was a widow with children living in different cities.
- She loved the house she was preparing to sell.
- She was financially able to maintain a large property.
- She was outgoing and enjoyed entertaining.

These clues helped Indie prepare for her first meeting with Ima, and also gave her a head start in knowing how to relate to this new client. Since Ima shared her high I traits, she was confident that they would get along well.

When Ima opened the door to Indie's knock the next morning, she greeted her with a warm smile and immediately took both of Indie's hands in hers.

"Oh, I just couldn't wait for you to get here. Come on, let's have some coffee and I'll tell you all about the house."

Ima, who appeared to be in her mid-60s, was wearing a bright yellow jacket over a deep green dress that complemented her lightly tanned skin and short dark hair. Her accessories included oversized gold earrings, a chunky gold bracelet and several rings. Indie, dressed in a red shift, immediately felt at ease with the older woman.

As she followed Ima to the kitchen, Indie noted several things about the house. It had a very comfortable, welcoming atmosphere, and she sensed that the many guests who had been entertained there had felt at home. There wasn't any feeling of sterility, of being afraid to touch the furnishings. Quite the opposite, in fact. Indie smiled to herself at the stack of magazines haphazardly tossed onto a credenza, alongside what appeared to be several days' worth of mail, acknowledging that her home and office looked much the same.

Adding to the warmth of the home was the variety of colors throughout the rooms. Clearly Ima was not afraid to make a statement, and what Indie heard loud and clear was, "Come on in, relax, and stay awhile." The rooms were painted in different colors, with furniture arranged to encourage conversation. Bright throw pillows casually tossed onto sofas made her want to sink in for a nice long visit.

Ima chatted as they walked, pointing out framed photos along the way.

"These are my kids when they came home last Christmas. Oh, what a time we had! And here are my grandbabies, all four of them. The twins just turned three; they're my son's boys. And the girls each have a daughter."

In addition to family photos, Indie noticed plenty of pictures of some pretty well-known film industry folks. Ima had been right; she certainly could name names.

"Is this your husband?" she asked, pointing to a picture of Ima sitting with an attractive silver-haired man and an Academy Award winning director.

"Oh, that's my Sam," Ima replied. "Always a smile; always a joke. Made himself right at home with everyone he met."

Another high I, Indie guessed. This house must have been filled with laughter and fun.

After a two-hour meeting that included lots of personal and entertaining stories, Ima signed a contract giving Indie the exclusive listing for her house. Indie looked forward to the transaction, sure that she would learn many more stories and share many more cups of coffee as the deal progressed.

Indie was glad to be working with Ima. She felt so comfortable with her, and truly enjoyed hearing Ima's stories, learning first-hand the history of the property and getting a feel for her new client's expectations and needs.

Not everyone is like Indie, though. The truth is that working with an I can be challenging, exhausting and entertaining, to say the least, particularly if I isn't in your nature. For the most part, Influencers are easy to get along with because they are people-pleasers who also want to be liked. Not being liked is their biggest fear. The only caveat is that you may have to keep them on target because they're a bit prone to going off on tangents.

With that in mind, leave plenty of open time for meetings with your Influencer clients. They have a lot to say about just about everything. Remember how you wished your D client would lighten up? You just might miss that precision and focus when showing listings to an I, who may recount stories of their day or the chronicles of their past based on whatever inspires them at the moment. High Is love to talk about themselves. You certainly won't be bored. Influencers are entertaining and fun, and they want to share and socialize and hear from you, too.

Don't try to cut the interactions short; allow plenty of time for stimulating, sociable activity. The high I buyer is going to require extra time because they need to toss around ideas. They are going to want you to participate in verbal exchanges, and yes, they like affirmation of their perspective and position. They crave personal attention and function best in a favorable and friendly environment. The Influencer is someone you just might spend time with long after you've closed their real estate deal. In fact, they'll probably invite you over to see the place once they've moved in. When you're selling to an I, say things like, "Can't you just see yourself entertaining in this kitchen?"

When you receive a call from a high I about a house they're interested in, they will probably go on and on about why they love the neighborhood, tell you that they used to live in the area or always wanted to live there, etc. While they will give you a lot of the info you need without you having to ask for it, they also may be hard to keep on point. Let them talk, and then ask the questions you need to if they aren't offering those details. "What's your price range?" "How long ago did you live in the area?" "Did you know that house has undergone several upgrades in the last two years?"

When you give information to your Influencer client, it's best to give it in writing as well as verbally; they might miss something because they move and talk so fast. You might prefer to communicate with them by email instead of phone, in order to minimize time spent talking. There's no need to dwell on the details with this client either, just keep them in the loop and let them know you're working on things. Is don't like wasted time and, like Ds, they want to see that effort is being made and time saved.

The challenge most high Is present is that they may appear a bit erratic and disorganized. You know the type − messy office, piles of papers on the desk. Don't be deceived by appearances, though, because they know exactly where everything is in that "mess." If your I client is a seller, expect their house to be slightly disorganized. You'll also need extra time when getting this listing because a high I will want to tell you stories about the house. Ask them for information to include in the brochures realtors put in each house, too. Is love those brochures.

In addition to your I client's personality traits, you'll also have to factor in their age. Though they may have much in common, there are still distinct differences among Is who are Baby Boomers, Gen Xers or part of Generation Y. Just as with each personality type, you'll have to adapt to each age group in order to develop the best possible working relationship.

For example, although Indie and Ima have a lot in common based on their personalities, their generational differences will affect the way they interact. As a member of Generation X, Indie is completely comfortable with email, text and instant messages. In fact, sometimes it seems that the only time she talks with friends or clients her own age is when they are actually face-to-face; everything else is done primarily by text and email.

Ima, on the other hand, is an older Baby Boomer about thirty years Indie's senior. She is accustomed to writing letters and notes and talking on the phone. She would rather have a friendly conversation than trade emails, which she considers too impersonal. Besides, she really isn't interested in learning new technology at this point; she can't understand how her children can stand using those smart phones and electronic readers.

In dealing with an I client of Ima's generation, you may well have to spend a bit more time on the phone than you normally would. However, balancing her I with her age, it's also a good idea to back up your conversations with written reports, since a high I may not pay attention to every detail you give them verbally.

Gen X and Y clients, on the other hand, will almost definitely prefer emails to phone calls. They may text you with questions as well. And those who are high Is will probably send you more than one message a day. Unlike more introverted types, Is are less likely to make a list of all their questions or ideas to minimize contact, and more likely to fire them out as they think of them.

Communication isn't the only thing affected by a client's generation. Their age and the era in which they grew up will also factor in to what they are looking for in a new home – or how they feel about selling their current home.

The majority of older Baby Boomers, those between 55 and 64, are interested in downsizing to a property that requires less maintenance. Buyers in this group are considering retirement and making plans for the rest of their lives. They value hard work and success; those with high I traits will want to share their life and career stories with you. Listen to what they say, even if it seems they are talking about unrelated matters. If you've been paying attention for the last couple of chapters, you know that those stories will help you to determine what they are really looking for. The person who raised his family in a house with a swimming pool and big yard will appreciate a development with a pool and enough outdoor space to enjoy. Younger boomers, those aged 46 to 54, are working hard to secure their futures. Those who have lost equity in their homes are concerned about having enough money for retirement; some may plan to continue working well past traditional retirement age. The Is among this group may openly express their concerns about needing to get their asking price, and will most likely want to discuss ideas and possibilities to enhance the sale.

Many in this age group still have children living at home, and may be paying tuition or planning weddings. If their kids are away at school, they may be concerned about whether they'll come back home to live after graduation. Be prepared for your I clients to want to toss around several scenarios that cover all bases. By listening closely to the ideas they return to most often, you can help them narrow down their list of "must haves."

Clients who are part of Generation X are entering peak earning years. Having grown up with technology, they value information and feedback. Perhaps because they've also grown up with exposure to news and tabloid stories about scams and scandals, they are skeptical and may question your estimate of a property's value. A high I Xer may have lots of stories about deals gone bad or friends who lost money in real estate. Don't take this personally; instead, use it as an opportunity to strengthen the relationship. Offer sites where they can do their own research to see that your information is correct.

A high I in this group will expect a fairly casual working relationship. As much as they love to talk, they'll also want to feel comfortable sending you quick messages and questions; just be prepared to talk more about them the next time you meet. Lifestyle and location are important to this group. An I will want to discuss architectural details, floor plans and layouts. They'll tell you all about their plans for their new home and will welcome your ideas and thoughts.

You may not have many clients from Generation Y yet – after all, they are 15 to 32 years old – although those on the higher end are up and coming in the real estate market. Mainly the offspring of Baby Boomers, many Ys are children of privilege – if not in terms of money, at least in terms of positive reinforcement and a sense of autonomy. Though many Ys rent instead of buy homes, they still value the things they are used to, such as modern amenities and technology-ready, energy-efficient homes.

A high I Generation Y client may have lots of stories about the way they grew up, the type of home they lived in, the way their parents did things. In general, probably because of their reliance on technology to communicate, this group as a whole lacks social skills. No matter how difficult it may be to be patient, don't talk down to them. Use action words and challenges; talk to them about tax advantages and building equity. You'll most likely experience the greatest generational difference with Ys overall. Listening to their stories and concerns will help you to find out what they need.

By now you're learning that so many of an individual's actions and words, in addition to their generation, contribute to clues about their personality. When you recognize those clues and identify the personality, your job and your life will be so much easier. I'm not saying you're going to like everyone you meet or that people won't still annoy you on some level. You'll simply accept them better when you chalk their behavior up to their innate personality style.

Let's do a quick recap of the Influencer to make sure you're up to speed on what to look for: Remember that 11 percent of the population falls into this category.

Classic I Traits:

- Outgoing and enthusiastic; enjoy being the center of attention; influence and inspire
- Excited by ideas, will offer opinions
- Greatest asset – fun to be around
- Greatest challenge – can appear erratic and disorganized
- Greatest fear – not being liked
- Need reinforced, friendly environment
- Use lots of expansive gestures and dress in bright colors

What the I Wants:

- Personal attention
- To be kept informed; submit information in writing
- Recognition for abilities
- To discuss ideas and options

Dealing with an I

- Let them talk, then ask questions to keep them on target
- Allow extra time for meetings to allow them to verbalize thoughts
- Ask questions that elicit feelings ("Can't you just picture your kids in this playroom?")
- Allow them some degree of intimacy (e.g., a two-handed handshake)
- Follow up conversations with written reports to be sure they get all information

Typical occupations of an I

- Actor / Entertainer
- Sales
- Bartender

Famous I Personalities

- Carol Burnett
- Bill Cosby
- Ronald Reagan
- Theodore Roosevelt

Chapter 5
THE RELATOR

So, are we having fun yet? I'm sure you never expected a book designed to help you better relate to people and be a more successful realtor to be this entertaining. To me, that's what your business should be, though. When you enjoy what you do every day to make a living – when you like your job – work isn't work. Not hard work, anyway. Really, who wants to work harder? Knowing how to relate to people on the level *they* want to be related to will make you smarter in your people skills and make your work so much easier.

As a real estate agent, you've got to like interacting with people at least a little bit. You also need interest in and appreciation for various styles of houses. How much more fun your job will be when you start identifying people's personalities, discovering their wants and needs before they actually verbalize the specifics to you, and matching them with the perfect home! It's much more than a game of chance and your prize at the end isn't exactly Monopoly money either. In addition to that financial fulfillment, you also have the personal satisfaction of knowing at the conclusion of a sale that you've helped another client achieve their goal. Hopefully, you've also made them a long-term client who will refer others to you.

Here's something very important for you to remember: Can you guess what the number one complaint about salespeople is? You've probably uttered it yourself if you've ever gone shopping for a new car or a major appliance. Yup. *They talk too much.*

Here's why that's a problem. If you are spending too much time as a salesperson *talking*, then you're probably not *asking* a lot of questions, which also means you aren't *listening.* You need to ask questions that get your client talking, while you listen and learn what they need. **He who asks the questions holds the power.**

As your client answers your questions, pay close attention to their style – do they talk with their hands, look you in the eye, pause and answer slowly? Observe *how* they respond, in addition to listening to *what* they respond, then adapt to that style.

Since we're on the subject of how to relate to people, we can smoothly transition into conversation about the next personality type in our DIRT acronym. The Relator is all about relationships and process, and, in fact, is the personality type of the majority of the population, though it may not be their only style. Most people will usually fall into the higher or lower end of the spectrum of their given personality style, and display a secondary style in addition to their more dominant personality. We'll learn more about how to identify and adapt to blends of personality styles a little later.

At the moment, you'll do well to recognize Relators, since about 69 percent of all people display classic Relator traits. These are genial individuals who like stability more than risk. They approach life in a steady and secure manner, and don't like to be rushed or hurried or pressured. Relators are also very much interested in their relationships with others. They are easy to get along with, dislike conflict and are "people people," meaning they are supportive and the ones you can always rely on. If each personality style had a motto in life, the Relator's would be, "Family and friends come first."

Relators are true team players and make excellent assistants, teachers, nurses. They thrive on productive routine, with the emphasis on constancy and steadiness. No drastic, dramatic or sudden changes for

Relators. Their demeanor is generally calm, which is the way they like the atmosphere around them to be. Relators are not big fans of change; in fact, they avoid it as best they can whenever they can, making them quite the challenge when it comes to buying or selling a house. Talk about change!

Relators will give you some obvious physical insight into their style, if you look closely enough. They won't shrink away from your touch, and though they'll shake your hand, it won't be with the firm grip of the Director. Relators are a bit more tentative and gentle in grasp and greeting. Eye contact is more intermittent than fixed, and movements are slow rather than animated and fast-paced.

You've probably picked up on the clue in his name alone that identifies Relan as the Relator in our fictitious real estate deal. Though I'd love to say that the story is factual and based on one of my own transactions, sadly that's not the case. I still have my imagination, though.

You'll recall that Relan is Mr. Driver's assistant, yet to our realtor, Indie, he appears to factor highly in the decision-making process regarding the Drivers' new home. Relan is the one who first contacted Indie, not so unusual for an assistant. She found him to be pleasant and engaging, on more than just a business level. This is quite typical for the Relator personality, whose focus is on relationships with others.

Relan had numerous email exchanges with Indie prior to the meeting. In addition to hammering out logistics, this type of interaction offered Relan some level of connection with Indie prior to their meeting. It gave him security and assurance as opposed to the uncomfortable feeling of meeting a stranger in a strange place.

Relators like reassurance and validation of their role and place. As Indie interacts more with Relan, she'll have to navigate his personality, making him comfortable with both their personal interaction and the professional process. Changes are about to occur in the lives of the Drivers, for sure, and if Relan is the key player she suspects he is, she'll have to outline the business process slowly and carefully for him, letting him know that she'll be there every step of the way for support.

When Ima Partay left the table, Indie noticed that Relan looked momentarily disappointed. She had briefly introduced Ima to the whole group and Relan had been the only one who greeted her warmly and with a smile. "Just as he did with me," Indie noted.

Relan appeared easy to get along with, although unlike Indie, he seemed more reserved and tentative. He smiled often, and had been polite and almost friendly throughout lunch, glancing at Indie during their limited conversation, though not holding her gaze.

As he dabbed at his chin with his napkin, Relan declared that the shrimp scampi he'd just consumed was indeed the best he'd ever sampled. "You should know, dear," Thea smiled, "you order it almost everywhere we go!"

That's why he barely glanced at the menu, Indie noted to herself. "I like to keep things simple," Relan said sheepishly.

"Well, if I ever get to come here again, I'll have to remember to order the shrimp scampi," Indie said, cheerily and supportively.

Indie could tell that Relan had questions, though he seemed reluctant to voice them. She made it a point to pause after offering information, allowing him to absorb it all and then ask if he or the Drivers had any questions or concerns. When he did ask questions, it was in a reserved, almost shy manner, not demanding or intrusive. And Indie didn't get the impression that Mr. Driver was annoyed, as he'd been with the waiter and Ima. In fact, Mr. Diver was oddly tolerant of Relan's exchanges with her and almost encouraged them.

She guessed Relan to be in his early 30s at the most, and she got the sense that he would probably be more sociable in more relaxed and friendly circumstances. He'd received and responded to several texts and emails during their meeting, and Indie wondered if they were business or personal. He briefly updated Mr. Driver after some of the messages, so clearly some were business related. Talk about a working lunch. She wondered if his Blackberry wasn't the perfect prop to keep him from having to interact too directly with the others. If they'd met in a social setting, Indie knew that she would have tried to draw him out in order to learn more about him.

Indie also noted how Relan took his time reviewing each listing she'd passed around to her clients. He had taken notes on everything Indie said, even though the information was all on the printed data sheets, which he kept in his possession. "Would you happen to have a 3-D virtual tour of any of these houses you've been showing us?" Relan asked. "I couldn't help notice the iPad in your briefcase," he added, not quite looking at her.

"Of course. I'm so glad you asked," Indie smiled and slipped the iPad out of its case, delighted to show off the features of the houses she'd selected.

"Do you have other houses on here in addition to those you just showed us?" Relan asked. Indie found it curious that Relan, not either of the Drivers, asked that question. "Can you show us some of the surrounding areas?" Indie nodded, narrowing the selection to only those houses with separate guest quarters, since this had been an earlier prerequisite. For the next 30 minutes she pulled up screen after screen, touring houses and neighborhoods.

Relan's interest was most piqued when viewing the landscaping and backyard areas, particularly the swimming pools and spas. "Are you an avid swimmer?" Indie hesitantly asked. Relan was the assistant, and didn't seem to be the one to whom she should be directing questions. He seemed very pleased, though, that she had shown an interest in him as a person and revealed that he'd been a competitive swimmer, still belonged to a swim team and elaborated on his passion for all things water-related.

"And they're moving to California. Hmmm, who's making the decisions here?" Indie wondered silently. She told Relan she'd just read an article about the top-rated adult swim teams in the area and would get him information about that and local yacht clubs.

"Would we be able to visit any of the houses that aren't in this folder?" Relan asked tentatively. "I don't want to upset your schedule and mess up the whole process." Indie assured him that it would be fine to add a few more houses to their expedition; she explained that all she had to do was make a couple of phone calls so that everyone involved would be prepared. In her gut, she knew she had picked the best and most suitable houses, and Relan's request to view the others seemed like more of a deterrent to their quest. She didn't mind taking the time, though she thought his selection of homes to see was rather random. The fact that Mr. Driver clearly disliked wasting time made Relan's request – and Mr. Driver's apparent acceptance of it – all the more puzzling.

65

By their very nature, Relators are not quite as clear-cut to identify as the Influencer or Director. They still have distinct characteristics that give them away. Let's see what clues Relan's left for us to follow.

- He greeted Ima warmly.
- He seemed disappointed when she left.
- He smiled often.
- He was reserved and tentative.
- He did not maintain eye contact.
- He often ordered the same meal.
- He asked a lot of questions.
- He took his time reviewing each listing.
- He took many notes.
- He wanted to view more houses.
- He asked about surrounding areas and neighborhoods.
- He was pleased that Indie showed interest in him as a person.
- He did not want to upset Indie's process.

Now, let's take a look at what Indie, the realtor who knows how to relate, did to make her client comfortable.

- She gave Relan time to absorb the details.
- She recognized that he was reluctant to ask questions.
- She frequently paused to ask if he had any questions.
- She took an interest in his personal interests.
- She offered to find ways for him to pursue the things he is accustomed to doing.
- She accommodated his request to look at more houses.

The most important thing you can do for a Relator personality type is create a favorable, safe environment. This is what Indie is trying to do for Relan. With her offer to get him information about swim clubs, she is giving him assurances that he is okay – and that she is going to be there to help him. That's how you need to address the concerns of the Relators you're working with, whether they are buying or selling. They need to know that you are committed to working with and for them to find the right home or the right buyer and to iron out any problems that may arise.

And you know that problems always arise. A smooth, flawless real estate transaction is the goal; the reality is that most people, buyers, sellers and realtors, don't get to that goal very often. Hitches and glitches abound in this world of listings, loan applications, appraisals, inspections, approvals. The best thing you can do for your high R personality is assure and reassure. Don't placate them, though. Explain the process and procedures. High Rs are easy to get along with, and they want to know that they are valued and they very much want a productive routine and relationship.

Many realtors say their number one frustration in working with a Relator personality is the inability to satisfy all of the buyer's needs. Then, the buyer turns around and buys from someone else – another realtor. Sound familiar?

While the Relator may be a difficult one to satisfy, if you change your approach in relating to them, you might end up with a more productive outcome for both of you. Remember, you are not going to change someone else's personality. You are not going to make your Relator client more comfortable with the fact that they are going to experience a major change; your high Rs are not going to freely verbalize their wants or concerns. Avoid losing the sale or the listing by saying and doing things to accommodate their style.

Ask more questions. Ask directly, "How many bedrooms do you want?" "What kind of square footage are you looking for?" "How big a backyard area do you want?" Repeat and elaborate on the questions to get as much information as you need to clarify their needs. This process will also help the high R clarify their needs to themselves as well as help them slowly adapt to the changes being thrust upon them. Once you go through this process thoroughly, you can use their answers to find what they are really looking for. Once they trust you and feel comfortable, they will share and open up and be a loyal client, forever.

The tricky thing about Relators is that, as much as they want to be liked, as easygoing as they can be, they do not like change. A high R is very resistant to it, and this trait makes it very difficult for them to make a decision. Rather than deal with trying to decide between options, they will stick with the norm. In our story above, the tell-tale sign of Relan's personality is his choice of the same or similar menu items from one dining establishment to the next. He doesn't want to have to make a decision, doesn't like change very much and is most comfortable with people and things he is familiar with.

I myself have a good friend who is well-off financially and a professional business woman, yet she rented a duplex for 25 years before buying a house because she was so reluctant and fearful of changes.

You know the type, I'm sure. That client to whom you show 42 different homes and she still hasn't written an offer? Now, I am not trash-talking this type of client. Every personality has its drawbacks. In this business, however, you have to be prepared to spend that kind of time on a high R client or you are going to be one frustrated realtor with nothing to show at the end of six months of traipsing from one house to the next.

This type of buyer is probably very nice. I dealt with one woman who was 49 years old and had never owned a home. She was very concerned about location, safety and what others thought of the home and location. She couldn't decide whether she wanted a condo or a single family home. So we looked at both, forever!

When we finally found one that she liked, it was in a community about 20 minutes from where she currently lived and where her friends were. Before she wrote the offer, she had to consult with friends to make sure they would come and visit. She had to check out many details about the home and area. This woman was a high R (with a secondary T, which we'll talk about in the next chapter). She had quite the difficult time making decisions and was very concerned about safety, as well as family and friends.

Identifying a high R in person is easier than doing so over the phone. When you get a caller with a Relator personality, they may be soft spoken and speak slowly. They may also talk about their families. To make future interactions with them easier, allow for this type of conversation, while also asking the caller exactly what they're looking for in a house to get more info. Then ask more questions to clarify their needs. For example, "You mentioned that you have three children and want a house with four bedrooms. This house has three bedrooms and an extra room for an office, does that work for you?"

Sometimes the attention to detail that a Relator type displays is really just a diversion from having to make a decision. This buyer will find something wrong with this house and something else in that house that doesn't quite fit what they're looking for. When you find what you think is the perfect match based on what they've told you, they may even alter what they previously listed as their objectives.

When working with a Relator, try to set some parameters for them. Tell them you understand how difficult the decision to move must be and find out what they would most need to have a successful outcome. What are their "must haves?" Allow your buyer to pinpoint the three things that are deal breakers for their perfect house.

Then allow them a few "nice to haves." These are things that are not necessarily deal breakers. They would serve as good swaying factors in the buyer's decision. Doing this helps the high R focus on what's important to them. Otherwise, they will railroad themselves, creating diversions, putting one obstacle after another in the way of making a decision. If this happens, Relators will start nit-picking, making mountains of molehills, which pretty much indicates they don't really want to move.

Remember the Top Three list. Hint, this works with all styles, except the High D. The buyer can only have three homes on their list to choose from. If you've shown five homes, two didn't make it to the top three. This will help your client to stay focused and not get too confused. Frankly, I can get confused myself after showing 42 properties! Something I do with all buyers is play the "name the house game," where each house is given a name. For example, in "the Parrot House" there was a talking parrot in a cage. "The Pink Bathroom House" had pink tile that the wife loved and the husband said had to go. It's fun and it helps people remember the homes. By the way, the buyer ended up buying "the Parrot House."

Relating to Relators of different generations involves patience and empathy on your part. For high R Baby Boomers, today's housing market may make it difficult for some to remain in their homes. Combine the forced relocation with their fear of change, and you've got the makings of a very traumatic and emotional transaction. If you're dealing with a very high R type, they may even be timid, repressing their concerns, not wanting to upset anyone. You'll need to put yourself in their shoes to see those concerns, and then encourage them to ask questions and verbalize what they want or need.

Highlight the benefits of the changes that will take place in their lives with a move. No more going up and down stairs to do the laundry; tell them real-life scenarios of other people who have gone through what they are and are living happily in the retirement community they're about to move into. Walk them through the process from listing to closing, and everything in-between.

Be open and direct, though, not blunt or cut and dry. Present R Boomers with just enough options to show you are flexible and they still have choices in their life; too many options, though, will just further delay the process. Try incorporating a little humor into your approach with R Boomers, which does not mean to make fun of them. Try to lighten up the atmosphere so they feel more at ease.

Relator personalities of Generation X (RXers) have largely benefitted from being children of the cyber age. Though natural introverts, they can communicate well through email, text messaging and social media. The natural trepidation with which they approach life may not be as apparent, thanks to the advances in technological communication. Intimate interaction can still be had without prolonged face-to-face conversation.

Be aware that it is still very important to treat RXers the way they need to be treated. Respect their questions by answering them. How many times have you sent emails requesting specific information, only to get a reply that does not address the answers you were seeking? This is a frustrating common practice in today's society and high Rs will take it personally, feeling foolish or offended if their questions aren't answered. When you send an email, in addition to responding to their business-related questions, ask about their kids, the trip they just went on or anything else personal that they may have shared with you. Staying in touch with your RX client regularly by phone or email will help them feel connected to you and valued as a client, which, of course, they are. Your job is to make sure they know this.

The Y Generation is actually buying homes earlier than their predecessors, probably due to the below-market values and federal tax credits. Accentuate these positives with Relators of Generation Y to make them feel more assured of their position and comfortable with making a purchase. They are the collaborators. They may buy a home together with others and live together; not like the communes of the '60s, but more to share the expense of the investment.

Your YR clients need positive reinforcement and a positive attitude, both because of their introverted personality type and because they are growing up in a challenging economy. What they want and value in a home isn't necessarily what they will be able to get. The YR wants the move-in-condition house with modern, technological amenities and energy efficiency. As his realtor, you may have to do some digging to find that out, though.

Because your YR client is Internet savvy, they may call you about dozens of houses they've seen online, appearing eager to buy. In reality, if they are a high R, they may actually be subconsciously sabotaging themselves by putting too many options on the table and being unable to make a decision. If you recognize this as their realtor, you'll be able to save time and frustration for you and your client.

Even if your client knows what he wants, this type of investment is likely a huge departure from the norm for the young Generation Y. This is where the fear of change and difficulty in making a decision kick in for YRs, and where you have to provide assurances. Go over their reasons for the move with them so they can refocus on their goal. To ease the decision-making process, narrow down the selection of homes based on their "must have" preferences. Then promise to be there throughout the entire process to answer questions, keep them up to speed and address any problems. Your YR clients need to know that you'll be there for them professionally and that you care about them personally.

Classic R Traits:

- Tentative in their approach
- Often brings family members to help in the decision process
- More introverted
- Gentle handshake
- Intermittent eye contact
- Slower movement and a steady pace
- Very patient; will take time making a decision
- Avoids risk
- Does not like change

What the R Wants

- A favorable, safe environment
- Information about neighborhoods
- Reassurance to know they're okay
- A checklist of the process
- A productive routine
- They don't always know what they want – a lot of "what if" scenarios

Dealing with an R

- Express genuine interest in them and their family (learn kids' names, etc.)
- Assure them that you will give them support throughout the process
- Acknowledge their concerns and provide support (don't make them feel they're asking dumb questions)
- Say things like, "That's a great question"
- Show them the process will be relaxed and pleasant (though sometimes it isn't in real estate, assure then you'll do your best)
- Remind them of the process repeatedly (the inspection is done, next we'll ask the seller to make repairs, etc.)
- Allow extra time with them, especially if they are first-time buyers
- Narrow down the properties to help them make a decision
- Find out if anyone else will be helping them make the decision

Typical Occupations of an R

- 69 percent of population
- Teacher
- Nurse
- Social worker

Famous R Personalities

- Mary Tyler Moore
- Mr. Rodgers
- Gerald Ford
- Dwight D. Eisenhower

Chapter 6
THE THINKER

Of the four people involved in our real estate transaction, Thea Driver is clearly the quietest. Indie, our P.I., recognizes Mrs. Driver as a Thinker, someone who is very conscientious and deliberate in her approach to life. As a high T, she loves process and procedure; order is very important to her. Many Thinkers work in careers where meticulous attention to detail is valued highly, such as accounting, engineering, law enforcement and the military.

Like most high Thinker personalities, Mrs. Driver produces quality work. A successful fashion designer, she does nothing halfway, and is as meticulous about the way her work is done as she is about the finished product. However, all of that conscientious attention can have a down side as well. Because of her strong need for excellence in all she does, Thea is prone to self-criticism. This trait can be very difficult for someone like her to overcome due to the high level of pressure she puts on herself to succeed, and to do so in precisely the way she has determined she should.

That critical trait can become a real stumbling block for people with predominantly high T personalities. Their concern about making a mistake or veering off course can prevent them from moving forward with a project. In many cases, this will spill out into criticism of others as well, making it potentially difficult to work closely with a Thinker. Acknowledging their inherent need for order will go a long way toward keeping things in balance.

Perhaps it isn't surprising that, given their strong need for order and detail, the greatest fear of high Ts is irrationality. They trust data, and prefer to do their own research to ensure that they have facts they can trust. While assembling their own data and keeping their own records appeases Thinkers, it may also cause them to get bogged down in the details and hamper their ability to make a decision. Not able to see the forest for the trees, as it were.

It also follows that a Thinker does not like surprises. Unexpected turns of events disrupt their sense of order and can throw a high T into a state of panic and self-criticism. Like the majority of high Ts, Mrs. Driver is an introvert. She appears shy and doesn't make a great deal of eye contact, although she is nevertheless gathering and storing the information she receives from Indie.

Thea Driver was seated between her husband and Relan. A tycoon herself, she appeared quite comfortable in her lush surroundings, though her contribution to the conversation taking place at the isolated corner table was limited. Not that she was disinterested; quite to the contrary, she appeared to take everything in, listening closely to every minute detail, even the waiter's in-depth descriptions of special menu items.

Although Indie dealt regularly with high-end clients and felt quite comfortable among the rich and richer, she was nevertheless impressed by the Drivers. She couldn't help noticing the brilliant glint from the flawless diamond on Mrs. Driver's ring finger as a ray of sunlight caught it just perfectly through the glass window. Yet she had to acknowledge that the ring, like everything else about Thea, was tasteful and understated.

The Drivers clearly handled their impressive wealth with class and elegance. Indie recognized that Thea's shoes alone cost more than some people pay in monthly rent, yet the woman was not at all flashy and didn't seem impressed with herself — perhaps more notably, she didn't seem to be trying to impress anyone else. Her meticulous appearance matched that of her husband, although neither seemed inclined to flaunt their wealth. Like her husband, Thea wore a simple suit that was most impressive for its obvious high quality and exquisite workmanship.

According to the information she'd dug up on them, the Drivers had been married for twenty years and by all accounts, appeared to be happy together. At least, there were no headlines or photos on Google indicating the contrary. In fact, there were very few headlines or photos of the Drivers at all...

As Indie described the properties she had selected to show to the Drivers, Thea listened attentively, nodding occasionally as her husband asked questions, taking notes in a small moleskin journal she took from her purse. When Indie finished with her descriptions, she asked Mrs. Driver if she had any questions. Anticipating that the older woman would be interested in the aesthetics of the properties, she was surprised when Thea asked very specific questions about the rest of the process involved in their transaction. Rather than details about the houses, she was more interested in the steps that would need to be taken to close on whichever property they chose, wanting to know about the title search, inspection and closing process. Indie carefully outlined each part of the process, assuring Mrs. Driver that she would keep her updated every step of the way.

Given Thea's interest in the transaction details, Indie was surprised by the woman's next request.

"Tell me more about the guesthouses, please. I'd like to know the particulars – square footage, amenities – and if you have printed floor plans I'd appreciate seeing them."

"Of course, Mrs. Driver," Indie replied as she reached into her briefcase for a folder. Knowing that the Drivers were intent on a property with a guesthouse, she had prepared a separate file with detailed information on each of the structures. She noted that although her iPad demonstration had included tours of several guesthouses, Thea wanted hard copies of the information. Clearly she was assembling her own file on the properties she was most interested in, and Indie made a point of recording precisely which documents she gave to Thea so she could be prepared to discuss the properties and answer any questions.

Mrs. Driver glanced at her husband, then turned to his assistant and said, "Relan, we'll have a look at these later today."

For Indie, the intrigue surrounding this deal continued to deepen. Having already identified Thea as a high T, she was nonplussed by the other woman's request for details about the process of purchasing a new home. What did surprise her was that, while Thea showed little interest in the details of her potential new home, she was singly focused on the particulars of that mysterious deal breaker, the guesthouse.

Thea's interaction with Relan formed another piece of the puzzle. She appeared very much at ease with the young man and seemed to know him well, more so than Indie would expect in a business relationship. Given his participation in the meeting, it was clear that he acted as more than merely a business assistant, yet Thea's comfort with him was nonetheless curious. Although she found Thea to be pleasant and personable, Indie was a bit thrown off by the other woman's limited eye contact. Though Relan shared a similar feature, she found him more approachable than Thea, who only looked fleetingly at Indie when asking a question, maintaining contact for just a moment. As she listened to Indie's responses, her eyes remained primarily focused on her notebook.

For an Influencer like Indie, it was a little unsettling not to have someone's full attention. Yet her experience told her that although Thea was greatly interested in everything going on at the table, she was naturally introverted and had difficulty appearing fully engaged in the conversation.

Our P.I. knew better than to underestimate Mrs. Driver based on her shyness, however. Though she may have been an introvert, Thea Driver was no shrinking violet. In fact, her orderly, logical mind was behind a wildly successful line of couture clothing for mature women. Indie had read a rare interview in which Thea, who had a background in fashion and retail, discussed the frustration her older clients felt trying to find age-appropriate attire in a youth-dominated culture. Recognizing a niche, she began designing clothing for that market, and now offered the collection in her stores in Palm Springs, Aspen, Boca Raton, New York and Chicago.

The interview Indie had read really was an anomaly. She knew that despite their wealth and prominence, the Drivers managed to keep themselves out of the news. While Mr. Driver's business dealings were often reported on, coverage of their social life was *primarily limited to their attendance at charity functions. They were a scandal-free couple, and now that she knew more about them, Indie wasn't at all surprised. As someone who needs to maintain control, it wasn't unusual that Mr. Driver would ensure that his reputation was untarnished by questionable behavior. In addition, he was primarily a businessman and wasn't involved in the regular goings on of Aspen society; Indie imagined that he would maintain the same low profile in Beverly Hills.*

Indie found Thea more of a curiosity, however. Despite her distinguished clientele of socialites and stars, many of whom she knew personally, there was very little coverage of her comings and goings. What Indie didn't yet know was that Mrs. Driver had her own reasons for avoiding publicity.

Let's take a break to consider the clues we've picked up this time around. Looking back at what you've read about Thea Driver, so far we know that:

- She was not talkative.
- She paid close attention to detail.
- She did not maintain strong eye contact.
- She was not flashy or ostentatious, in spite of great wealth.
- She was interested in the details of the real estate transaction.
- She wanted hard copies of information for her records.
- She seemed very comfortable with Relan.
- She was a successful businesswoman.
- She avoided publicity.

And how did Indie respond to the clues she picked up about Thea?

- She recognized Thea's shyness.
- She gave her the specific details she needed about the transaction.
- She understood Thea's need for order and details.
- She provided the documentation Thea wanted.
- She asked if Thea had any questions.
- She thoroughly explained the process and promised to keep Thea updated.

As she has done with the other members of the group, Indie uses the clues Thea unconsciously gives to find the best way to interact with her during their transaction. She knows that deciphering those clues is her key to striking the right note with Thea.

It's clear to Indie that Thea is going to assemble her own file of properties. She knows that in addition to the paperwork she has provided, Thea will most likely do her own research to satisfy her need for order and process. She doesn't distrust Indie's abilities; she simply needs to reassure herself that every possible step of the process has been completed.

Indie is able to assemble her clues by observing Thea in person. Talking on the phone with a Thinker will also provide clues, although you may have to work a bit harder to find them. Similarly to a Director, high T callers will ask for details without offering any information about themselves. Give the caller the information they want, and ask some subtle questions to elicit more information. "Is this in your price range?" "This home has four bedrooms; does that match your needs?" And be sure to ask if the caller has any additional questions before ending the call.

When you work with a Thinker client, whether a buyer or seller, practice patience at all times. There's no doubt that it can be a bit frustrating to have to revisit each part of the transaction again and again, yet this client may very well need to do just that. A high T wants to know that nothing has changed to upset the progress of the deal. Remember that Thinkers don't like change, which is the basis of any real estate transaction. Whether they are buying or selling a home, your Thinker client is facing a huge life change, and their dislike of that fact will lead them to think and rethink every aspect of the deal. That penchant for over-thinking can lead to a high T getting stuck on their way to making a decision; you may have to be a bit persistent to get them back on track.

Though we all strive for problem-free real estate deals, the fact is that too often, something unexpected pops up to throw a monkey wrench into the works. When your client is a Thinker, you'll have to tread very carefully when the unexpected occurs. High Ts need to be reassured that you'll do everything possible to prevent surprises along the way. If you can't avoid one, however, explain the possible outcomes and assure the client that you are working hard to keep things on track.

If your Thinker client is a buyer, they'll want to know all about the business end of the deal, just as Thea does. Sellers will have the same concerns, and will also worry about whether the buyer's financing is secure and if you have a back-up plan in case it isn't. In either case, allow the client to ask the questions they need to in order to feel confident about working with you.

One of the most valuable skills you can practice with a Thinker is diplomacy. High T personalities want to know that they are right, that their intense thought process has paid off. Show appreciation for your client's accuracy and attention to the process. It can be easy for someone who doesn't share these traits to lose patience with a high T's seemingly endless need for details; recognizing this will help you to establish a good relationship with your client.

This is something I wish I'd been able to communicate to my husband during a recent visit to a home improvement company. My husband is a contractor who has rented products from this company many times. The owner of the company offered to help us, and instructed another customer service representative to call a janitorial company to verify exactly what we needed to accomplish our task. It was New Year's Eve and not very many businesses were open; of course, the janitorial company was one of those that were closed.

My husband assured the woman that he was comfortable with the equipment, having used it several times. Unfortunately, she wasn't comfortable with taking his word for it, and insisted that we had to speak with someone who knew about the floor buffer.

I sensed that my husband was losing patience; after all, he knew what he knew, he just couldn't get this woman to understand that. While I could see his growing agitation, I was also aware of the owner's discomfort. Despite her persistence, she seemed to find it difficult to maintain eye contact with us, looking from one to the other and frequently down at her computer screen.

After several more minutes of conversation, we persuaded the owner that we had used the machine previously and were confident in our ability to use it again. Although we did convince her of that, she still insisted on explaining the process step by step, and even went so far as to make us turn the machine on and try it out right there in the store.

At this point I could sense that my husband was approaching the boiling point, although he would never have shown it. When we were finally on our way home with the buffer, he said, "That woman was driving me crazy!"

While I could certainly sympathize (we are both High Is), I explained that the owner was a high T, a Thinker who needed to be sure that she'd followed every step of the process she was accustomed to.

"I don't like it when people do that to me. I'm a contractor; I know what I'm doing!" my husband insisted.

"Yes, I know that," I replied, "and you know that. The point is that she didn't. She *had* to go through her steps. She had to ensure that she showed you everything she needed to, or she would have felt that she'd left out something important."

The moral of the story is that I knew we had to allow the woman to show us how to use the machine. If I had been able to point this out while in the store, my husband would have been more understanding, even though frustrated. After all, he is a P.I. in training.

As with the other three personality types, generational differences also impact the way you'll relate to your Thinker clients. We've already talked about the fact that many Baby Boomers involved in real estate transactions are preparing to downsize and may be giving up the home where they raised their families. Like Relators, Thinkers are averse to change, and the thought of making such a move at this stage in their lives can be downright frightening.

High T Boomers have most likely lived in the same home for a long time and will have difficulty envisioning themselves anywhere else. Downsizing may also necessitate getting rid of some of their possessions, which can also be hard for them to face. Encourage this type of client with positive talk about the simplicity and ease of life in their new home; point out the advantages of a smaller yard to maintain, or a cozier area for family gatherings.

Younger Thinkers, those of Generation X, will be most comfortable communicating through email and texting based on their inherent shyness and introversion. While they may be uncomfortable with personal meetings, they will be able to share their concerns with you through technology. This brings up an important point. Communicating by email and text has many advantages – speed of delivery and response are high on the list. Yet in spite of the upside, this type of communication has also made us susceptible to the curse of responding too quickly. It's so easy to dash off a quick reply to a client's question, though many times that's not the right thing to do. While clients do want quick answers, they also want complete answers. Particularly high Ts.

If you receive an email asking about the client's closing, don't respond with just the time and place. Take the time to explain the process; give the client the details you know they need to ease their mind about what lies ahead. Closings can be fraught with emotion, and anything you can do to relieve your high T client of anxiety will only serve to make the proceeding that much smoother.

In addition to the information you provide, your TX client will want to do their own research. Allow time to discuss what they present, and show appreciation for the time and effort they've spent on the research. Be diplomatic at all times; if their research has essentially duplicated what you've already provided, it's best not to point that out. Simply acknowledge their effort and move along.

Like other members of Gen Y, your client will most likely want a home on a relatively small lot that doesn't require a lot of upkeep, and will probably be most interested in walkable communities that are close to where they work. They want outdoor space, though not necessarily the huge yards they may have grown up with, and like such amenities as fitness centers and party rooms where they can entertain guests. A TY client will want to discuss all the advantages and disadvantages of a specific property. Since this is most likely their first real estate transaction, be prepared to carefully answer many questions about the art of the deal.

Since Thinkers make up only 17 percent of the population, they may be the most difficult for some people to work with simply by virtue of the fact that they aren't encountered that frequently. To be fair to your Thinker client, you might want to consider telling the other participants in the transaction about their personality. For example, letting the title company and lenders know a bit about the client's needs will give them a heads-up toward helping the client with the least amount of frustration and allowing more time for the closing. This is in no way a denigration of Thinkers; on the contrary, it's really a way of keeping them happy throughout the process. In fact, I have given high T clients their contract way in advance of making the offer, just so they have time to read it over and see if they have any questions.

Remember that it's your job to make your client feel comfortable and confident. Once you've found the clues you need to identify the Thinker, be patient, diplomatic and persistent to get them talking about what they really need. With those clues and your abilities as a P.I., you'll be able to help them achieve their goals.

Classic T Traits:

- Limited eye contact; tentative handshake
- Dislike surprises
- Interested in data
- Need to conduct their own research
- May get bogged down in details and have difficulty making decisions
- Excited by reason and order
- Their greatest asset is producing high-quality work
- Their greatest failing is being too critical, often of themselves
- Their greatest fear is irrationality

What T Wants

- To be reassured that there will be few surprises
- To be kept fully informed of the process
- To keep their own records
- To feel that they are right
- To be appreciated for their accuracy

Dealing with a T

- Be patient and diplomatic
- Allow them to do their own research, even if it is repetitive
- Keep them apprised of every step in the process
- Let other participants know the client's needs
- Show appreciation for their input
- Ask questions to keep them focused

Typical occupations of a T

- 17 percent of population
- Engineer
- Accountant
- Librarian
- Law enforcement
- Military

Famous T Personalities

- Mr. Spock
- Sherlock Holmes
- Felix Unger
- Albert Einstein

Chapter 7
SECONDARY
PERSONALITY STYLES

Before you start thinking that you now know everything you need to know about the four different personality types, I've still got a few P.I. tips under my trench coat to share with you. I can almost hear your question: "If the acronym for the four different personality types is DIRT, and we've already analyzed the Director, the Influencer, the Relator and the Thinker, what are we missing?"

A lot, actually. As much as we'd all probably like for people to be that precise, for their personalities to be cut and dried, we know better. We can't just place people in their assigned box and tie them up with a pretty bow. "You're a Thinker." "He's an Influencer." And so on. Human behavior doesn't quite work like that. Identifying and subsequently relating to different personality types is a science, though not in the same emotionally detached way as diagnosing and treating a condition or symptom is a science.

As you hone the personality identification skills you've acquired, you'll crack the code to actions and words that give away a person's inherent personality. What happens, though, when you catch that person exhibiting a trait not generally associated with the personality you identified? While it's, of course, a possibility that you incorrectly interpreted the clues, it's much more likely that there's a secondary personality coming into play. I'm not talking Sybil here – multiple personality disorder. That's an entirely different scenario. A secondary personality means that an individual has some traits associated with a personality type that differs from their more dominant one. Most people, in fact, have a dominant and a secondary personality style.

Have you ever gotten to know someone, think you've pretty much got them figured out, and then they say or do something that surprises you? Something that you perceive as totally out of character for them? Instead of thinking that you had them all wrong, consider that in a given situation or setting, their less dominant personality takes control. The classic scenario of the quiet office co-worker who dances on the table at the company party comes to mind. While that's an extreme example, environment is certainly one thing that can trigger an individual's less prevailing personality. Circumstances are another. Sometimes, unfamiliar situations make a person uncomfortable and their natural reaction is to behave in a way different from what is considered normal for them.

Oddly enough, genetics evidently has little to do with a person's dominant personality. How often does a parent lament or rejoice in the fact that their child is nothing like them? "I was never that confident or outgoing when I was her age," or "I don't know how he came to be such a perfectionist." When it comes to that auxiliary personality, though, environment and surroundings may have a lot to do with its emergence.

Take the gruff, all-business high D CEO, like our Mr. Driver, for example. His natural personality seems to be a perfect fit for the competitive industry he's involved in. His lack of patience and tolerance at lunch further prove that Indie's assessment of him as a firm and determined force to be reckoned with is dead on. His behavior at their meeting is typical of his inherent personality because he is comfortable in this type of setting. He's a successful businessman; he conducts important business transactions over expensive lunches. This is his world and he feels a sense of comfort and belonging here.

Yet, his patience and even deference to Mrs. Driver while she asks questions of Indie, and even of Relan's interactions with the realtor, reveal a hint that there's more to Mr. Driver's persona than meets the eye.

Indie asked Mr. Driver if he would mind her taking a few moments to make some phone calls and reconfigure their house-viewing schedule in light of the unexpected additions that Relan and Mrs. Driver requested.

"I want to map out the most efficient route possible, since I know how valuable your time is," she said. Mr. Driver smiled gratefully at what Indie assumed was the fact that she acknowledged the importance of his time. He nodded slightly at Relan and patted Thea's hand tenderly.

"Indie, I am afraid that I have broken one of my own cardinal rules and must apologize to you," he began.

Indie looked quizzically at him, though she had a feeling deep inside that she was about to learn what she had suspected right from the start. Something more was going on here than she was aware of.

Mr. Driver continued, "Time is indeed a most valued commodity to me, as I sense it is to you as well. By not giving you all the information you needed, I may have wasted precious ticks on both of our behalves."

Indie resisted the urge to interject, tell him that she was sure their time had been well-spent regardless, and point out all that had been accomplished at their lengthy luncheon. She also suppressed a witty, though cutting comment that might have been suitable if a friend had kept her waiting and wasted her time; in this case, however, it would be impetuous and inappropriate. She remained silent, the slight hint of a smile on her lips, a question in her eyes, glancing at Thea and Relan, both of whom avoided her gaze.

Mr. Driver cleared his throat, clearly uncomfortable in his present role. The man could control a meeting, indeed an entire roomful of people with his direct and to-the-point manner. The information he was about to give Indie now, though, was of a highly personal nature and he hadn't been prepared to share it. He silently admonished

89

himself for that, knowing that he had to be willing to make this sudden change in order to have a successful outcome. Disclosing the details would place them all on the most productive and purposeful path; it was a risk he had to – was willing to – take.

"I am extraordinarily impressed with each of the houses you originally selected to show us," Mr. Driver began. "Based on what you know about us – on what we've told you about us – any one of them would be most suitable. I am also most appreciative of your patience in our requests to view other listings. I'm sure you are curious as to why."

"A house is a very personal decision, not to mention a major financial investment, Mr. Driver," Indie remarked. "You have every right to see as many houses as you'd like in order to find the one that's the best fit for you and Mrs. Driver…and Relan," she tentatively added.

Across the table, Relan couldn't help smiling broadly.

"Indeed, we do have that right. What we don't have is the right to keep something from you that prevents you from doing your job to the best of your ability. I don't want you to think that you haven't done the very best research you could in finding us the right home," Mr. Driver said. Indie could tell that he must be a very motivating man to work for.

Mr. Driver reached over to pick up the folder containing the photos and listing information for all of the houses they'd decided to view. "Every piece of information I could ask for is contained in these printouts. Every style of house that your expertise and research indicates would appeal to Thea and me is right here. A job very well done."

"Except that I'm missing something," Indie said, feeling oddly comfortable with Mr. Driver on a personal level and unsettled on a professional one.

"You're missing something that you didn't have, not something you overlooked," Relan interjected. "There's a tremendous difference."

Indie appreciated the vote of confidence. "I would welcome the information much more," she thought silently.

"Well, for heaven's sake," Thea Driver said hesitantly, "This poor woman knows no more now than she did when she sat down at this table. While I am still at odds with myself about it, I believe that it's time to tell Indie what she needs to know. It's either that or we spend two months looking at every possible house to suit any possible taste, lifestyle or individual, which would be a colossal waste of time…

"My dear, this is all largely my doing," Mrs. Driver added, glancing at Indie. She hardly seemed to be the determining factor or force in her marriage, and Indie was intrigued that she was the one taking responsibility. *"Relan and my darling husband go to great lengths to take care of and protect me…and to meet my stubborn demands. I think this time, though, I was a bit extreme, and have probably set this whole process behind a great deal."*

Indie felt compelled to say something; Mrs. Driver seemed to be feeling so conflicted and discouraged. *"Oh, Mrs. Driver, please don't fret about this. There are much more dreadful ways for me to waste my time than having lunch here with all of you,"* the joke spilling out of her mouth before she could stop it. Her objective had been to try to allay the woman's concerns, and she hoped Mrs. Driver took her words with the levity with which they were intended. She certainly didn't mean to offend her in any way.

Relan laughed aloud and Indie cast him a grateful look as she breathed a sigh of relief. The table went suddenly silent, with no one sure of what to say next. Indie could tell that whatever the information was that they felt was so important to share, they certainly did not **want** to share it. She struggled to come up with some way to make it easier for them, realizing that over the course of their multiple-hour lunch, she was coming to know these people on a deeper, more personal level. She had pegged them fairly well from the start, yet in these last ten minutes, she was getting more than a glimpse into their secondary personalities, which, along with the yet-to-be-revealed missing information, would only help her to better assist her clients.

It was Relan who quietly spoke up first, and from the looks on their faces, even Mr. and Mrs. Driver were surprised by that. *"You are very witty and very charming, Indie, and obviously quite good at your job. It's just that we have conducted our business in the same way and under the same premise for so long that it's difficult to change it now. If we're going to get anywhere, though, we need to bring you into the loop. To say that I would rather not would be an understatement; unfortunately, I see no other way."*

"To be honest, I knew there was something more going on here," she ventured hesitantly, not sure where she was going. It was Mr. Driver who stunned her by cutting her off. *"Well, why didn't you say something? We could have cleared all this up an hour ago."* She drew a sharp breath, then exhaled with a grin when she saw that Mr. Driver was wearing a grin of his own. *Now Indie knew that the comment was*

meant in a friendly, almost humorous way, though a lesser P.I. might have thought he was being condescending.

"I just wanted to keep things strictly business and professional, the way I thought you would want them," she smiled at him.

"In any other business situation, you would be most correct," Mr. Driver nodded. "This time, with this house, business is a bit more personal."

You are probably as curious as our fictional realtor to learn the mystery of the Drivers' real estate needs. All good things come to those who wait – and continue to read. Indie is getting clues into the auxiliary personalities of her clients by the boatload. She's also leaving clues of her own into her secondary style. Before we unravel our fictitious tale, let's dig deeper into our characters. Let's begin with Mr. Driver:

Clues:

- He smiled gratefully at Indie.
- He patted Mrs. Driver's hand.
- He apologized to Indie for not giving her all the information she needed.
- He appeared uncomfortable in this situation.
- He was struggling with taking what he considered to be a risk.
- He praised Indie for doing a good job.
- He displayed a sense of humor.

Now, knowing what we do about Mr. Driver, some of these clues fit right in with his high D personality. He takes control of the situation; something he seems to be quite accustomed to, on both a personal and professional level. Yet, he exhibits gratitude, remorse, tenderness and even humor, which are not traits normally displayed by the Director type. At least, not outwardly.

Another personality style is emerging from the shadows of the more dominant high D. This style has some of the attributes – and drawbacks – of the Relator personality. Mr. Driver is the type that doggedly perseveres to achieve his goals. That type of determination indicates that the proper information is necessary, so he knows he has to come clean with Indie, though it's an inner struggle to do so. He has to respond quickly to that inner challenge and demonstrate an ability to be flexible in his approach. He knows Indie has been working her best and because he appreciates that type of dedication, knows she might be frustrated.

A high D with a secondary R is an Attainer and an Achiever. He is a versatile self-starter who works hard, is organized and goal-oriented, and knows where he is going. He also possesses the ability to motivate others to use their skills, which is what makes him a successful businessman and good employer.

Classic D/R Traits:

The strengths of the D/R:

- They are the most subdued of the extrovert personality types.
- They accomplish many tasks.
- They know where they are going.
- They are organized.
- They are hard workers.
- They have the ability to motivate others to use their skills.

The weaknesses of the D/R:

- You are never sure when they are joking.
- They have a cutting tongue.
- They don't change their minds easily.
- They are more worrisome than other D types.

The D/I is an Influencer/Concluder. They tend to be logical, critical and incisive in their approach to attaining goals. D/Is seek authority and challenges and they accomplish goals through people. When under pressure, D/Is may be blunt and critical.

Classic D/I Traits:

The strengths of the D/I:

- They are extreme extroverts who love activity.
- They are purposeful, productive promoters.
- They thrive on challenges.
- They are the best motivators of people.
- They are convincing debaters.

The weaknesses of the D/I:

- They can be hostile.
- Their anger is explosive.
- They are impatient.
- They are sarcastic, opinionated, impetuous and manipulative.
- They have a razor-sharp tongue.

The D/T is the Challenger/Confronter. The high D with the secondary traits of the Thinker personality acts positively and directly in the face of opposition. These are forceful individuals who will take a stand and fight for their position. They are willing to make changes and may overstep authority.

Classic D/T Traits:

The strengths of the D/T:

- They are industrious and capable.
- They are a combination of optimism and faith.
- They like goals and details.
- They are thorough leaders.
- They have quick and analytical minds.

The weaknesses of the D/T:

- They like an argument.
- They are opinionated.
- They can be sarcastic.
- They may harbor hostility and resentment.
- They tend to focus on tasks rather than people.

Next up is our realtor with attitude, Indie. A high I to be sure, though she does have a few traits in common with Mr. Driver, of all people. We've listed clues in the previous chapter addressing the Influencer, now where does Indie show hints of the D lurking beneath?

Clues:

- She wanted to map out the most efficient route to view houses.
- She was determined to do what it takes to find the house the Drivers are looking for.
- She wisely held her tongue when Mr. Driver admitted that he hadn't given her all the information she needed.
- She let words slip that she may not have said aloud in other professional circumstances.
- She did not get upset or insulted.
- She kept things strictly business, because she knew that would appeal to Mr. Driver.

Indie is a Persuader/Convincer. An I/D tends to behave in a poised, cordial manner, displaying "social aggressiveness" in situations that he or she perceives as favorable and unthreatening. This is why she let her guard down and allowed the Influencer in her to make that joke to Mrs. Driver. The I/D exudes charm and strives to establish rapport, even at first contact with others. They also accomplish goals through people.

Classic I/D Traits:

The strengths of the I/D:

- They are the strongest of the extrovert personality types.
- They are enthusiastic.
- They possess the charisma of the I along with the resolution of the D.
- They are very productive individuals.

The weaknesses of the I/D:

- They talk too much.
- They sometimes expose weaknesses.
- They are complimentary, though at times cutting and insulting.

A high I with a secondary R is the Advisor/Counselor. They tend to seek out people with enthusiasm and spark. An I/R is outgoing, displays a contagious optimism and tries to win people through persuasiveness and emotional appeal.

Classic I/R Traits:

The strengths of the I/R:

- They are easy to like.
- They make delightful co-workers.
- They have a happy, carefree spirit.
- They are helpful; understanding and good listeners.

The weaknesses of the I/R:

- They lack follow-through.
- They are disorganized.
- They lack discipline.
- They would rather socialize than work.
- They are overly tolerant with non-producers.

A high I with a secondary T is the Accessor/Teacher. They display self-confidence in most endeavors with others and are always striving to win people over. The I/T is reluctant to give their own point of view. Regardless of obstacles, I/Ts feel able to act in order to attain success.

Classic I/T Traits:

The strengths of the I/T:

- They are highly emotional.
- They are willing to promote the projects of others as well as their own.
- They are good public speakers.
- They are creative.

The weaknesses of the I/T:

- They are dreamers.
- They are often fearful.
- They sometimes have a self-condemning attitude.
- They sometimes have problems with anger.
- They are overly critical.

The Relator personality, you may recall, represents the vast majority of people. Detecting their secondary style is a huge benefit in distinguishing how to relate to them and meet their needs. In the passage above, Relan doesn't offer too much, and both what he does and does not do helps to reveal the rest of his personality.

Clues:

- He avoided Indie's gaze.
- He smiled, visibly happy that Indie had acknowledged him in the housing decision.
- He pointed out to Indie that she had not overlooked information; rather, she had not been given it.
- It was out of character for him to speak up.
- He was calm even though he was negative about sharing information.

The R/I is an Advocate/Agent. They tend to be controlled and patient and move with moderation and deliberateness in most of their undertakings. Even under stress, R/Is will usually project a relatively unruffled appearance. They generally approach most situations with care and concentration.

Classic R/I Traits:

The strengths of the R/I:

- They are easy to get along with.
- They are congenial, happy and people-oriented.
- They are diplomatic.
- They are fun-loving and humorous.
- They are good administrators.

The weaknesses of the R/I:

- They are lax in motivation and discipline.
- They are conservative about how much effort they put forth.
- They can be fearful and insecure.

While Relan is a close fit for an Influencer as his secondary style, it's difficult to imagine that Mr. Driver would hire an individual who is lax in motivation and discipline as his assistant. And, he's not been exactly fun-loving and humorous, though he is on a working lunch.

He appears to be more of the Relator with the Thinker as his secondary style. This R/T is the Peacemaker/Diplomat. These individuals tend to be persistent and persevering people who are not easily swayed once their mind has been made up. They set their own pace and follow a very precise system. R/Ts can be rigidly independent when force is applied, exasperating others who want them to adapt or change. Remember how Relan essentially orders the same meal when he dines out. In this most recent passage, he is gracious to Indie, approaches the situation passively and methodically, and admits to feeling negative

Classic R/T Traits:

The strengths of the R/T:

- They are gracious.
- They are gentle and quiet in nature.
- They resist aggression of any kind.
- They are rarely angry or hostile.
- They are dependable.
- They are exact, neat and passive.

The weaknesses of the R/T:

- They can be fearful.
- They are sometimes selfish.
- They can be negative.
- They are critical.

about it.

The R/D is the Attainer/Achiever. They are normally steady and consistent individuals who prefer to deal with one assignment at a time. An R with a D auxiliary will usually direct skills and experience into areas requiring depth and specialization. They are steady under most

Classic R/D Traits:

The strengths of the R/D:

- They are the most active and fast moving R type.
- They are good under pressure.
- They are practical.
- They don't like to venture beyond the norm.
- They give sound advice and make good counselors.

The weaknesses of the R/D:

- They can be stubborn at times.
- They are unyielding.
- They can be fearful.
- They sometimes refuse to cooperate.
- They are selfish about their personal life.

pressures and strive to stabilize their environment.

The last blend of combinations deals with the Thinker personality. Let's

Clues:

- She was at odds with herself about telling Indie the truth.
- She felt badly about wasting all of their time.
- She admitted that her husband and Relan are protective of her.
- She took responsibility for the situation.

take a look at some of the clues Mrs. Driver gives into her secondary style:

Mrs. Driver is probably closest to the T/R, or Precisionist/Perfectionist. She exhibits a precise, detailed and stable nature, though she is concerned with avoiding risk or trouble. T/Rs are systematic thinkers who tend to follow procedures in both personal and work life.

Classic T/R Traits:

The strengths of the T/R:

- They are great scholars.
- They are organized and analytical.
- They are good-natured and conscientious.
- They are detail-oriented and accurate.

The weaknesses of the T/R:

- They are easily discouraged.
- They are negative thinkers.
- They are prone to depressive thoughts.
- They may experience inner turmoil.
- They can be stubborn.

They act in a highly tactful, diplomatic manner and rarely antagonize.

The T/D is known as the Designer/Administrator. This person tends to act in a careful, conservative manner and is reluctant to compromise position in order to achieve goals. A strict adherer to policy, they may appear rigid in following a set rule or formula. A T/D prefers an

Classic T/D Traits:

The strengths of the T/D:

- They can be both a perfectionist and a driver.
- They have the facts and the ambition.
- They are very prepared and well-organized.

The weaknesses of the T/D:

- They can be difficult to get along with.
- They are rarely satisfied with themselves.
- They are prone to criticism and bitterness.
- They find it hard to forgive.
- They show intense anger.
- They can be "nitpickers."
- They show their disapproval.

atmosphere free from antagonism and desires harmony.

The Thinker with a secondary personality of an Influencer is an Assessor/Reviewer. They are sticklers for systems and order. A T/I makes decisions based on proven precedent and known facts. They try to meticulously meet standards that have been established, either by

Classic T/I Traits:

The strengths of the T/I:

- They make wonderfully gifted classroom teachers.
- They are fact-oriented as well as relational.
- They are low-pressure people.
- They are not very adventurous.

The weaknesses of the T/I:

- They display big mood swings.
- They are highly emotional.
- They can be self-pitying.
- They analyze things too much.
- They are highly critical and often rigid.
- They may have a poor self-concept.

themselves or by others. They can articulate data with great effectiveness.

You have probably had your own special clients whose real estate needs seemed to be a mystery. No matter how many houses you showed them that met the criteria they'd given you, they just couldn't find the right one. Remember, how you deal with your clients is just as important as the houses you show them. Maybe some part of them isn't giving you everything you need to know to help them find everything they want and need in a home. If you relate to them on a deeper level and peel back the layers, they may reveal something more about who they are and what they want. When you get really adept at personality identification and can assess a person's secondary style, you'll be amazed at how successfully you'll be able to relate to them. Assuming, of course, that you are willing to adapt. That's crucial. Figuring out who a person is, how they act and react is fun all by itself; remember that your purpose here is to use it as a tool for your business success.

Chapter 8
CLEANING UP WITH DIRT

Y ou can see how the combination of primary and secondary personality styles adds a whole new dimension to the DIRT system. Now that you've learned a bit about those secondary styles, you're entering into the advanced level of P.I. training. Recognizing secondary styles will be invaluable when you encounter a client who presents traits that seem contrary to their primary personality, as Indie has done with the Drivers and Relan.

Let's let Indie off the hook and see exactly what lies at the bottom of this intriguing transaction.

With every word spoken by the Drivers and Relan, Indie became more eager to know the truth about what they needed to tell her. Her mind was whirling with possibilities. Clearly Relan was a major factor in this deal, which had to mean that he was more than merely Mr. Driver's business assistant. What could that be?

Taking his wife's hand in his, Mr. Driver looked at Thea, who nodded. "It's time," she said. "I trust Indie; tell her."

"We know that our insistence on a guest house has been puzzling you, Indie," Mr. Driver began. "I'm sure you wonder why two people need a four-bedroom house

with a guest house and pool. I suppose I would wonder the same in your position."

Indie simply nodded, not wanting to interrupt Mr. Driver.

"We also know that you're very thorough and have researched us as well as the properties you want to show us. I'd expect nothing less from someone with your professional reputation. And I do know your reputation, because I've done my own research. The reality is that I've probably learned much more about you than you have about me, because Thea and I value a very private lifestyle."

"No kidding," Indie thought, acknowledging that the Drivers must trust her indeed. This incredibly private couple was about to reveal a secret, and clearly they were confident that she wouldn't run with it to TMZ or People magazine. Well, if she did, that would be the end of the sterling reputation Mr. Driver just mentioned…

"I think it's time to get to the point, dear," Thea interrupted. "They'll be wanting this table for dinner service soon," she smiled.

Indie smiled as well, and noticed that Relan seemed about to burst. Clearly he was as anxious to get this story told as she was to hear it.

Mr. Driver drew a breath and spoke quickly. "Very few people know that Relan is not only my assistant. In fact, this transaction is actually a family affair."

Indie couldn't completely hide her startled expression, glancing from Mr. Driver to Relan, who continued to grin. Aha, the plot thickens…

"My wife had a sister; sadly, she died many years ago when her only son was just a child. The boy's father had also passed away, and Thea became his guardian. This was when she was just getting her start as a designer, and she worked very hard to build her career and a life for her nephew. When I met her the boy was only seven, and she had just won the design contract that would launch her career."

As the pieces began to fall into place, Indie found herself imagining a young Thea Driver in the position her husband described. Surely her Thinker personality had been an asset in planning her own future and providing for her nephew, allowing her to carefully set a course of action that would benefit both of them.

Surprisingly, Thea spoke next. "I'm sure you've figured out that Relan is my nephew," she said, smiling warmly at the young man.

"I've been dying to tell you!" Relan interjected.

"Yes, I see that now," Indie replied. She added cautiously, "I don't understand why it's a secret, though."

"That's my doing," Thea answered. "As I told you, the men in my life are very protective and indulgent of me. When my sister died and Relan came to live with me, I promised myself that I'd give him the most normal life that I possibly could. The design job that put me on the map was huge, and the potential for publicity was enormous. I refused to allow Relan to be part of the craziness of the press, since I felt he'd already experienced more upsets than any child should. I never even mentioned him in interviews. In fact, I said very little about myself in order to protect him, and soon it became known that I never discussed my private life."

"Aunt Thea was amazing," Relan laughed, looking at Indie. "She worked so hard and made sure I was happy. As a kid, sometimes I'd even ask if I could be in a magazine or on the news with her, and she always said no, that it really wasn't any fun at all. I really did have a normal, happy childhood, which definitely would not have been possible if she'd let me have my way!"

Mr. Driver picked up the narrative. "When my wife and I married, we agreed that we would continue to keep Relan out of the public eye. And given our own natures, we weren't too eager for publicity ourselves. We've grown to value a level of anonymity that a lot of people in our position don't share. When Relan began to express an interest in business, he interned with my company. He exceeded my expectations to the point that I knew he was the best choice as my assistant. Since it's a privately owned company, there are no restrictions on family members working together."

Indie nodded and smiled. She could even see the family dynamic at work now, especially given all she knew about each member's personality. They complemented one another, and now that she was observing them on a personal level, Indie saw that they seemed very happy together.

Still, though, what did all of this have to do with the house? She decided to venture a guess.

"I truly appreciate your trusting me with the truth," she said, addressing her comment to all three. "And I assure you that no one will ever learn any of this from me," she smiled. Looking at Relan, she said, "So I guess you'll have the final say on *the guesthouse, since I assume you'll be moving in with your aunt and uncle."*

"You've got it almost right, Indie," replied Mr. Driver. "Relan will be moving with us, though not quite in the way you think. You see, you're also right about something else. Thea and I certainly don't need a four-bedroom house. We've spent the last twenty years in big homes, and we're ready to downsize. Relan, on the other hand, is just starting out. We thought it would be a good idea to find a place where he can raise a family and we can shed some of our extra baggage. Indie, my wife and I will be moving into the guesthouse. Relan will have the main house. With the large properties you've shown us, we'll be able to live together as a family and still each have privacy."

"I thought it was odd that Relan had so much input – no offense. Especially about the grounds and the swimming pools…" Indie's voice trailed off as she worried that perhaps she was talking too much and overcompensating for what she now perceived as missed clues.

"Please don't worry, Indie," Thea replied. "There's no offense taken. How could there be when we withheld so much from you? Your instincts were good."

Indie appreciated the reassurance. "It's a very logical decision," she said. "It will provide each of you with just what you need." As she looked around the table at her new clients, she added, "And please don't worry about not having told me this earlier. This has been a wonderful lunch and a fascinating meeting; I've learned more today than you could possibly imagine."

Indie's last statement is the truth. Her meeting with the Drivers and Relan has served as a crash refresher course for this PI. Although she already had top-notch skills, her new clients presented more of a challenge than she was accustomed to because they weren't forthcoming about their needs. As you've already learned in your own career, not every client will tell you everything you need to know. That's why you're learning to become a P.I., isn't it? So that you can see beyond the obvious and get to the root of what your client really needs.

As much as I hope you've enjoyed our fictional real estate deal, you already know that it isn't the reality of how most transactions go. It would certainly be nice to handle deals with wealthy clients in fancy restaurants. And it would also be nice if all of your clients offered as many clues as Indie's, even enough to let you know that you are missing information. The reality is that you don't always — perhaps, never — have the luxury of spending several hours observing clients first-hand, trying to decipher their personalities so that you can establish the best possible relationship.

Quite the contrary. In the real world, business is conducted in your office, at the kitchen table of a house you're showing, even in your car. Sometimes the majority of your communication is over the phone or through email, with only a few face-to-face meetings. I feel that it is important to have at least one face-to-face meeting with your important contacts, even if they aren't in a transaction with you. They are your referral base. Keeping in front of them increases the odds of getting referrals. Add to that the fact that you are hopefully handling multiple transactions simultaneously, and determining personality types can be tricky. It definitely can be done, though. You just need to observe what you can about your clients and fit the clues into our DIRT system; then you'll be able to figure out what your clients need and find the best way to help them achieve it.

As you've followed Indie's real estate deal, you've read a lot about digging up the DIRT on other people's personalities. Remember, though, that in Chapter 1 I told you the importance of knowing who you are in order to be a good Personality Identifier. And now I'm reminding you not to leave yourself out of the equation. It's so important to be aware of your own personality style; it's the critical first step in becoming a successful PI. Your self-awareness will enable you to more honestly assess your clients' personalities and figure out just how to accommodate their needs and expectations. Take another look at the assessment you filled out back when we started, to remind yourself of your personality type. You did do that, didn't you?

It's also important to remember that the four questions we've applied to each personality style apply to you as well. Identifying your style is one thing; fully understanding it is another. Whether you are a Director, Influencer, Relator or Thinker, ask yourself the questions you've read throughout this book. What excites you? What is your greatest asset? What is your greatest failing? What is your greatest fear? Answering these questions honestly will make it that much easier to understand how they help to define others.

Don't forget to factor in secondary styles, too, for yourself as well as others. Your secondary personality type can be a great help in finding the right way to approach a client. Perhaps you have a secondary D, which would help you to better understand Directors and Thinkers, both of whom appreciate efficiency and accuracy. If you are a D or T, a secondary I or R may soften the edges of your direct personality, making it easier for you to be more outgoing and expressive with Influencers and Relators.

Knowing your own personality, primary as well as secondary, will also help you to determine when it's best to refer a client to another agent. There are bound to be times when, despite your best efforts, you just can't make a connection with someone. Perhaps your styles are simply too different to find any middle ground; it's certainly possible. When this does happen, remember not to beat yourself up and take it personally. You won't be able to change the other person. You need to remember that they aren't judging you; they don't dislike you. No one is right or wrong. You just aren't a match. Trust your instincts and acknowledge that you won't be able to help them. You'll be doing them a service by referring them to an agent who is better suited to work with them; you'll be doing yourself a favor by removing yourself from a potentially negative relationship. You'll hopefully be doing a favor for the other realtor, who will, in turn, do a favor for you in the future.

As a realtor, you know that the deal doesn't end once your client's offer is accepted. In fact, you and your client are hardly the only people involved. In a successful real estate transaction, in addition to your client you'll be dealing with other realtors and perhaps the seller. The sale will also involve inspectors, appraisers, a title company, lenders, attorneys – there are a lot of i's to dot and t's to cross. In the case of a client with an extreme personality type, like a very high I or T, you might consider giving a heads-up to the others so they're aware that the client might need some extra time throughout the process (remember my engineer client who read the closing documents?). It will help the transactions go much more smoothly if everyone knows what to expect.

Chances are that you probably do this already. How many times have you told a colleague, "Be prepared; this client really likes to talk," or "Better have your info at your fingertips; you're going to get barraged with detailed questions." I doubt there's an office in the world, in any industry, where people don't do just that. Granted, information like this isn't always shared in the most flattering way. Again, don't judge. Now that you're becoming a skilled P.I., you know that the chatty client or the one who needs all those details addressed is simply behaving as their inherent personality dictates. You can still let others know what to expect – just be nice!

As we've discussed, generational differences work in tandem with personality types to determine what people need and expect and how they make decisions. Being objective and diplomatic with different generations may be hard at times; again, so much depends on your own age and personality. If you're a Boomer with a high I working with a client from Gen X or Y who is a high R, you might find it difficult not to see them as one of your own kids and want to guide them through their decisions. On the other hand, depending on your own secondary type, you may find yourself wanting to scold that young client for their seeming lack of social skills, such as texting the entire time you are explaining important details. Remember to take all the factors into consideration when deciding how best to approach a client.

Now that you've read about the four personality types, as well as the secondary traits that can impact a person's behavior, let's see how you fare as a PI. As you read the following stories, look for clues to help you identify each person's dominant style. When you're done, visit www. pesonalityidentifier.com to see whether you've nailed them.

Story 1:

Apharmacist called his computer technician because all of his data had been lost during a power surge. The technician bluntly told the pharmacist to get out his backups so the tech could restore the files.

The pharmacist hesitated. "Oh, well …"

"When is the last time you backed up the files?" the technician interrupted impatiently.

"Last week," the pharmacist replied sheepishly.

The technician was livid, and yelled into the phone, "How many times have you been told to back up every day? How am I supposed to help you without those files? Now you'll have to recreate all the prescriptions you've filled since your last backup. I can't believe you haven't learned this and done what I've told you to do!" In reality, this diatribe was laced with lots of expletives.

At this point, the pharmacist had become so upset that he was crying. For weeks, even months, he fumed over the way the technician treated him during the call, replaying it over and over in his mind. On the other hand, fifteen minutes after the call ended, the technician barely remembered it at all; he had no idea of the impact he'd had on the pharmacist.

Which personality type is the pharmacist?
What about the computer tech?

Story 2:

Sally is a young single woman who wants to buy her first home. When she finds a house she likes, she tells her realtor that she wants her father to see it, too. Dad shows up with a flashlight and tape measure and begins to nitpick every detail. He's nearly as thorough as an inspector, and asks lots of specific questions about insulation and the age of the roof. The look on Sally's face is sad; while she loves the house, if Dad doesn't approve, she isn't going to buy it. When her father finds fault with too many items, Sally tells her realtor that they have to keep looking and hopefully, her father will like the next one better.

Where do Sally and her father fit into the DIRT system?

(In this scenario, your P.I. skills should have told you that the buyer would probably want someone's input before making an offer. When you sense that this is the case, ask the buyer. This way you can be prepared to assess the second person's style as well and be ready with the information they'll need to make a decision.)

The next two stories feature characters with a primary and secondary personality style:

Story 1:

Margaret was a very nice woman in her 40s who had never owned a home. She was extremely concerned about location and safety, as well as what others would think of her choice. She couldn't decide whether she wanted a condo or a single family home, so her realtor spent weeks showing her both.

When they finally found one that Margaret liked, it was in a community just twenty minutes from where she currently lived, and where all of her friends and family were. Before making an offer she had to check out every detail about the area, and consult with her friends and relatives to make sure they would come to visit. Her meticulous attention to detail actually made it difficult for her to reach a decision; it took some pointed questions from the realtor to make Margaret realize that she already had all the information she required to make her choice.

Which primary personality type is Margaret?

What is her secondary style?

Story 2:

Awell-dressed woman walked into a large real estate office, and, without a word to anyone, sat at the loan officer's empty desk, took out her Blackberry and began texting. The staff in this friendly firm was taken aback. Whispers began circulating.

"Oh no! Is Bill being replaced? It had better not be by her!" they gasped.

The woman hadn't introduced herself or even acknowledged the existence of anyone in the office, which didn't instill a sense of goodwill in any of the agents or clerical staff. At last, one of the agents asked the manager who this rude stranger was, and learned that she was the owner/CEO of a large national mortgage bank who was in town for a visit with Bill's boss.

Now, this woman had come from New York to visit an office in the South, where things are naturally a bit more friendly and accommodating. When word got back to one of her vice presidents that the staff had been upset by her behavior, he told her that she should have introduced herself and established a rapport with the people she was visiting. She was surprised, since that was something she was not accustomed to doing; it had simply never occurred to her.

Can you identify the stranger's primary and secondary styles?

Okay, now let's take it up a notch. The stories that follow each involve two people, and each has a primary and secondary style. Good luck!

Story 1:

Ann was an excellent executive assistant. Her organizational skills were incredible and she had great rapport with all of the staff and the boss's colleagues. She was very dedicated, often working long hours to complete the job. Eager to please, she always smiled and asked others how they were. For Ann, family came first, and she considered her co-workers part of the family.

She also endured verbal abuse from her demanding boss, Fred, who blamed her for anything that went wrong, even things that were not her fault. He seldom acknowledged her accomplishments, and offered no emotional support or even a simple, "good job." To the contrary, Fred needed to be in charge and couldn't share the limelight with his assistant, regardless of how well she worked.

Ann began to feel that she constantly gave and never received any support or appreciation in return. Her resentment grew as she felt used by her demanding boss; she wondered if she could muster the courage to address her feelings with him.

How have you identified Ann and Fred's primary and secondary styles?

Story 2:

Bob was attracted to Linda's stunning beauty and intelligence, and loved that she could seemingly talk to anyone. He was not very sociable and didn't care at all about social functions, yet knew they were necessary to his business success. Linda would be an asset to both his personal and professional life.

Not only did they marry; they also became business partners. Bob was the technical visionary, dreaming up innovative ideas to implement for major market impact. He just lacked the ability to put the ideas into action, which was Linda's forte. She created impressive business plans and had the charisma to get the attention of investors and buyers.

Bob often drove clients and employees to tears, screaming at them and belittling them if he felt something did not meet his expectations. These incidents meant nothing to him; he barely remembered them once they were over. He was a workaholic who found it nearly impossible to relax, and, as time went on, Linda began going out with friends because her husband preferred to stay at home and work. Bob was unable to trust anyone else to complete tasks, and felt that too much time away from the office was too great a risk.

For Linda, the lack of support or any complimentary words from Bob became stifling. He didn't get her sense of humor; she could no longer tolerate his yelling and degrading comments. Their business success was not enough for her; she needed emotional support from her husband. Bob refused to seek counseling and Linda refused to be ignored. Sadly, the marriage ended.

What are Bob's primary and secondary traits?
What about Linda?

So, how did you do? Were you able to identify the personalities on display in these stories? By now you should have the skills to figure out the first two with ease. If you unlocked the combination styles as well, kudos!

Although the DIRT system will become second nature to you in a short time, until then it's perfectly acceptable to use a reminder when you need one. In the beginning it's easy to confuse the similar styles and forget the particulars of each – believe me, I did! When I first started using this system, I kept a cheat sheet near my phone. Whenever I answered a call, I referred to my list to see where the caller fit into the system. And it didn't take long at all before I was able to identify callers on my own. Check out the Appendix for a reference list that you can keep on hand as a reminder of the different styles.

As we reach the end of our lesson in personality identification, I hope you take away from this book an appreciation of just how valuable – and enjoyable – P.I. can be. It can have a positive impact on your relationships, both professional and personal, and it can successfully improve your business relationships and increase sales.

We began by stating some basic principles of our business. First, people do not buy things, they buy expectations. Second, it's important to maintain close contact with clients. Third, when two people really want to do business together, they won't let details stand in the way.

Using the DIRT system can help you to make the most of each of those three points. Especially in real estate, buyers' decisions are heavily influenced by expectations (don't forget, so are sellers'). By identifying personality styles, you will be able to recognize those expectations, and even help clients acknowledge things they may not be aware of. Knowing a client's personality will make it so much easier to maintain contact. You'll understand their communication style and be able to accommodate their needs. And finally, DIRT can help you to get beyond the pesky details that too often derail a business relationship.

As we look to the future of real estate, I'd like to leave you with a few thoughts. Decide where your interests lie and develop a niche. Specialization can be a great way of making a name for yourself. Whether it's relocation services, commercial sales, working with seniors, land development or any other aspect of the industry, becoming an expert in an area allows you to focus your energy on what you do best. Developing a niche will also help to focus your marketing, making your advertising more noticeable.

Marketing is important for generalists as well. Implement a plan to target the three generations that will make up the majority of the market over the next several years. Reach out to Baby Boomers, Gen X and Generation Y in ways that will appeal to each. Once you've attracted their attention, use the DIRT system to seal the deal.

If you haven't yet, learn all you can about technology. Become comfortable with social media; it's the way of the future – even the present – for more than half the clients out there. If this is something you've been resisting, now is the time to jump in and learn. It can be as easy as asking a young person you trust to teach you the ins and outs of Facebook and Twitter, as well as whatever else pops up!

Most importantly, remember the power of knowledge. Everything you learn will help advance your career. That's the purpose of this book, to teach you one of the most powerful tools you can employ throughout your career. It is my sincere hope that the knowledge you've gained here will serve you well, for a long time to come.

APPENDIX

Personality Assessment

In the 4 boxes below there are twenty adjectives. Think how each of the adjectives describes you. Check all that apply to you in each section.

Part 1

- [ ] Satisfied
- [ ] Patient
- [ ] Contented
- [ ] Sympathetic
- [ ] Neighborly
- [ ] Amiable
- [ ] Possessive
- [ ] Gentle
- [ ] Indirect
- [ ] Compatible
- [ ] Willing
- [ ] Kind
- [ ] Relaxed
- [ ] Loyal
- [ ] Controlled
- [ ] Complacent
- [ ] Warm Hearted
- [ ] Good Listener
- [ ] Cooperative
- [ ] Team Player

Part 2

- [ ] Outgoing
- [ ] Gregarious
- [ ] Poised
- [ ] Socializer
- [ ] Emotional
- [ ] Stimulating
- [ ] Playful
- [ ] Inspiring
- [ ] Entertaining
- [ ] Cluttered
- [ ] Persuasive
- [ ] Fashionable
- [ ] Trusting
- [ ] Expressive
- [ ] Influential
- [ ] Captivating
- [ ] Confident
- [ ] Enthusiastic
- [ ] Creative
- [ ] Fun

Part 3

- [ ] Compliant
- [ ] Correct
- [ ] Fussy
- [ ] Orderly
- [ ] Neat
- [ ] Reserved
- [ ] Conservative
- [ ] Humble
- [ ] Conventional
- [ ] Soft Spoken
- [ ] Careful
- [ ] Precise
- [ ] Agreeable
- [ ] Detailed
- [ ] Cautious
- [ ] Diplomatic
- [ ] Perfectionist
- [ ] Exacting
- [ ] Respectful
- [ ] Pleaser

Part 4

- [ ] Pioneering
- [ ] Self-reliant
- [ ] Positive
- [ ] Competitor
- [ ] Blunt
- [ ] Individualist
- [ ] Demanding
- [ ] Impatient
- [ ] Restlessness
- [ ] Assertive
- [ ] Determined
- [ ] Persistent
- [ ] Courageous
- [ ] Direct
- [ ] Adventurous
- [ ] Tenacious
- [ ] High-spirited
- [ ] Aggressive
- [ ] Outspoken
- [ ] Bold

Count the checks in each box above and record the totals on the next page.

The highest total is usually the one that best describes you.

Part 1	Part 2	Part 3	Part 4
Relator	**Influencer**	**Thinker**	**Director**

Now that you know what your style is, while you're reading the book look for the ways that your personality style contributes to your decision making and how you respond to others. Knowing your personality style through and through is your first step to becoming a great P.I.!

DIRT Quick Reference Chart

D	**I**	**R**	**T**
Director	**Influencer**	**Relator**	**Thinker**
WHAT	**WHO**	**WHY**	**HOW**
Want to make money, save time, be more efficient Be short and to the point-closed questions	Want to have fun, talk about themselves Add humor, don't labor details	Want security, safety, sense of belonging Ask for their opinion & feelings-open-ended questions	Want practicality, logic, fairness, systematic approach Give facts, documentation, data, printouts
SEEKS	**SEEKS**	**SEEKS**	**SEEKS**
Productivity, bottom line	Recognition, fun	Acceptance	Accuracy
FEARS	**FEARS**	**FEARS**	**FEARS**
Being taken advantage of	Loss of prestige	Sudden change	Criticism of work

RECOMMENDED READING

"Two of the most mentally stimulating activities a person can undertake are reading and writing. Make a commitment to read at least 30 minutes a day."

Cindy's Recommended Reading Baker's Dozen

1. The Platinum Rule – Tony Alessandra and Michael J. O'Connor
2. The Sales Professional's Idea a Day Guide – Tony Alessandra, Gregg Baron & Jim Cathcart
3. Snap Selling – Jill Konrath
4. Relationship Selling – Jim Cathcart
5. The Acorn Principle – Jim Cathcart
6. Little Gold Book of YES! Attitude – Jeffrey Gitomer
7. Tribes – Seth Godin
8. Tough Times Never Last-Tough People Do – Dr. Robert Schuller
9. Non Stop Networking – Andrea Nierenberg
10. Creating Customer Evangelist – Ben McConnell
11. Customer Mania! It's Never Too Late To Build a Customer-Focused Company – Ken Blanchard, Jim Ballard & Fred Finch
12. Referrals For A Lifetime – Ken Blanchard
13. Tipping Point – Malcolm Gladwell

ABOUT THE AUTHOR

As a sleuth with a sweet disposition, Cindy began her career in sales. Later she owned more than 15 successful companies, hosted a highly-rated talk show as well as trained sales professionals to become Personality Identifiers (P.I.s) in her unique program. Her clients have included Oklahoma Association of Realtors, IBM, Proctor and Gamble and a multitude of real estate companies. With an accomplished background in training, education and sales (with a few certifications to boot!) Cindy has become the premiere PI speaker, trainer and author.

She lives in Tulsa, OK with her husband Mark Salas, and their two rescue dogs, Norman and Lola.

Contact
Information

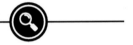

Want more information or to schedule a speaking engagement by Cindy Manchester?

Contact Cindy Manchester
Phone: 918-625-7441

Email: cindy@personalityidentifier.com or

Visit www.personalityidentifier.com for in-depth DIRT assessments and reports:
- Team Assessments
- Values Assessments
- Sales Styles
- Power DIRT